THE JUSTICE OF GOD

THE JUSTICE OF GOD

A Fresh Look at the Old Doctrine of Justification by Faith

James D. G. Dunn
and
Alan M. Suggate

William B. Eerdmans Publishing Company
Grand Rapids, Michigan

First published 1993 by the Paternoster Press
P.O. Box 300, Carlisle, Cumbria, CA3 0QS, UK

This edition published 1994
through special arrangement with Paternoster by
Wm. B. Eerdmans Publishing Co.
255 Jefferson Ave. S.E., Grand Rapids, Michigan 49503

Printed in the United States of America

00 99 98 97 96 95 94   7 6 5 4 3 2 1

Library of Congress Cataloging-in-Publication Data

Dunn, James D. G., 1939-
The justice of God: a fresh look at the old doctrine of justification by faith /
James D. G. Dunn and Alan M. Suggate.
p.   cm.
Originally published: Carlisle, Cumbria, UK: Paternoster Press, 1993.
Includes bibliographical references.
ISBN 0-8028-0797-6 (pbk.)
1. Justification — History of doctrines. 2. Christianity and justice.
I. Suggate, Alan M. II. Title.
BT764.2.D86 1994
234′.7 — dc20   94-16690
CIP

Contents

Introduction 1

PART ONE A Fresh Look at the Biblical Emphases 3

1 Martin Luther and the Individual Conscience 5
2 Justice for Gentiles: Paul and Justification by Faith 17
3 The Justice of God 31

PART TWO Three Case Studies 43

Introduction 45
4 Germany: A Tale of Two Kingdoms 49
5 Japan: Imperial Missions 61
6 Britain: Free Market and Faith 71

Conclusion 81

Questions for Discussion 83

Suggestions for Further Reading 85

Introduction

What is 'justice'? Most people would be happy with an answer in terms of 'fairness'. Justice is done when each receives his or her fair share or reward.

What is 'justification'? The word is much less familiar, but best known in Protestant circles, in the phrase 'justification by faith'. There it defines the doctrine that God accepts individuals as they trust in him and not on the basis of anything they do or have done.

What is the relation between the two? Most would find the question difficult to answer. But the definitions already given suggest that the two stand in some opposition. A doctrine which denies that acceptability to God depends on what individuals do seems to run counter to the idea of each receiving his or her fair share or reward.

The consequence is that very few have bothered to ask whether there is or should be a closer and more positive relation between justification and justice. The two have been allowed to become unrelated concepts. Justification has become confined to the sphere of religion and individual piety. Justice has become a matter for the state. The result is an unhealthy compartmentalizing of religion and social obligation.

But are the two concepts unrelated? Should justification by faith be so divorced from social justice? If instead of speaking of 'justice' we speak instead of '*God's* justice' what difference would that make? Does the rather dated Protestant talk of 'justification by faith' have more to say to contemporary needs and concerns than has been generally recognized?

These are some of the questions which lie behind this joint study. They emerged as the agenda for a study group set up to plan a sequel to *The Kingdom of God and North-East England* (London: SCM, 1986), under the auspices of the Scripture, Theology and Society Group of The Foundation for the Study of Christianity and Society. After several false starts the format agreed was that adopted in the following pages.

The first three chapters are written by James D.G. Dunn, Lightfoot Professor of Divinity at Durham University. In them the biblical foundations of the doctrine of justification by faith are examined afresh and a fuller understanding of justification brought to light in which the justice of God is shown to have national and social as well as individual outworkings.

The second part is written by Dr Alan Suggate, Lecturer in Theology at Durham University, who specializes in Christian Social Ethics. Three case studies show how serious have been the effects of a misunderstanding of justification and of a false separation between justification and justice, and indicate clearly how a fresh restatement of the interaction of justification and justice could have considerable and fruitful consequences for international and social justice.

PART ONE

A FRESH LOOK AT THE BIBLICAL EMPHASES

CHAPTER ONE

Martin Luther and the Individual Conscience

Some time in 1515 or 1516 Martin Luther made the great discovery out of which the Reformation was born. He discovered 'justification by faith' – a doctrine which has been at the heart of Protestant thinking ever since. It is not too much to claim that this single discovery decisively transformed European Christianity, and with it European history, both political and cultural. For it was this doctrine which led to Luther's break with the Church of Rome, and to church leaders and princes being forced to take sides for or against the Reformation, with all the consequences which followed. What was it that proved so important and had such effects?

Until that time Luther had been a devoted monk (of the Augustinian order), a gifted student (he earned his doctorate in 1512) and a devoted teacher of the Bible. The problem lay in his own spiritual life. He had no peace of heart, no quietness of conscience. The doctrine of human sinfulness depressed him, and no amount of penance and confession seemed able to remove his own sense of guilt before God. What he feared most of all was 'the justice of God'. By this he understood the anger and judgment of God against sinners. At that time, when life was often very short, the thought of death could be very frightening. For after death came the judgment. And for the guilty, hell loomed as a terrifying prospect.

But then came the great discovery as he wrestled with the words of Paul's letter to the Christians in Rome. The sticking point for him was Paul's talk of 'the justice of God' as revealed in the gospel (Romans 1:17). How could God's just punishment of sinners be 'gospel', that is, 'good news'? Let him tell his own story in his own words:

> I greatly longed to understand Paul's Epistle to the Romans and nothing stood in the way but that one expression, 'the justice of God', because I took it to mean that justice whereby God is just and deals justly in punishing the unjust. My situation was that, although an impeccable monk, I stood before God as a sinner troubled in conscience, and I had no confidence that my merit would please him. Therefore I did not love a just and angry God, but rather hated and murmured against him. Yet I clung to the dear Paul and had a great yearning to know what he meant.
>
> Night and day I pondered until I saw the connection between the justice of God and the statement that 'the just shall live by faith' [Romans 1:17]. Then I grasped that the justice of God is that righteousness by which through grace and sheer mercy God justifies us through faith. Thereupon I felt myself to be reborn and to have gone through open doors into paradise. The whole of Scripture took on a new meaning, and whereas before the 'justice of God' had filled me with hate, now it became to me inexpressibly sweet in greater love. This passage of Paul became to me a gate of heaven . . .
>
> [taken from Roland Bainton's *Here I Stand* (London: Hodder & Stoughton, 1951) p. 65, slightly adapted].

So, what does 'justification by faith' mean? What was Luther's great discovery? There was obviously an absolutely crucial shift in his understanding of God. It is summed up in the shift from talk of God's *justice* to talk of God *justifying*.

It is important to recognize that the language in all this is the language of the law court. Luther's problem had been the mediaeval Church's emphasis on God or Christ as judge. The whole of life on earth was but a preparation for that final court of judgment, presided over by the judge of all the world, which would settle where each person spent eternity. And there is no shortage of such talk in the Bible to feed such fears. We need think only of passages like Matthew 25:31–46, Mark 9:43–48, Romans 2:5–10 and 2 Corinthians 5:10.

The assumption, then, was that wherever the New Testament spoke about God's justice, it was God's verdict against sin and his sentence against the sinner which was in view. For anyone with an unquiet conscience, Bible readings on God's justice were a fearful experience.

The discovery which Luther made was twofold. First, that when Paul talks about God 'justifying', he had in mind not so much God's *condemnation* of sin as his *acquittal* of the sinner. The distinctive feature of the gospel is not what it says about God's justice in passing sentence on human wickedness. Rather, the distinctive feature is what the gospel says about God pardoning the wicked. The judge can also pronounce a verdict of 'Not guilty'.

This also means, secondly, that the law court metaphor could not be pressed, as though it was the only way of picturing God's attitude to his human creation. God was not only Judge, but also Father. And as in a family, relationships are not governed solely by strict rules, as though a judge continued to act only as a judge even in his own home and with his own family.

God is also kind and generous to his children. He accepts them as they are, with all their faults and failings. He welcomes the sinner, warts and all.

What Luther realized is of tremendous importance – that God's acceptance is the *beginning* of spiritual striving, not its *goal*. The light which dawned on Luther was that Christianity is *not* a matter of anxious striving for God's favour. It does not depend on our ability to please God. It is not to be thought of as a dogged discipline in hope of winning God's final commendation. Instead, Christianity *starts* from the recognition that we can *never* work our passage to heaven. This is not just because we could not succeed if we did try, but because reliance on our own effort turns us away from God. Christianity starts from the amazing discovery that 'God justifies the ungodly' (Romans 4:5). He is the God who offers to accept the wicked as they are, and starts renewing them from there.

That is a tremendously powerful grasp of the Christian gospel. No wonder it lit the fires of the Reformation in 16th century Europe. For countless thousands terrified of hell, dismayed by the prospects of purgatory, and put off by the abuses of the mediaeval church it was good news indeed. Christianity starts from the offer of God's unconditional grace – an offer extended to all, of whatever age, stage or condition.

The insight granted to Luther has remained at the heart of Protestant Christian thought. 'Justification by faith' is a sharp sword which punctures all inflated thoughts of self-importance. It is a sharp knife which cuts away all reliance on human effort, on human cleverness. It is a sharp spade which undermines any attempt to build our own protective barriers or control our own destiny. It cuts through all human pretence, all human self-assurance, all human boasting. God accepts not the important, or the activist, or the clever, or the powerful as such. It is the *sinner* he accepts. That is an insight which has been applied over and over again in Christian critique of false religiosity and political systems. It is an insight which must never be lost from the gospel.

Christianity starts with the sinner opening an empty hand to receive God's undeserved grace. It starts with Luther's recognition that God offers his acceptance as a free gift, the assurance that God's acceptance comes before and is far more important than anything we can do either for ourselves or for him.

There is more to it, of course. For example, in Christian thinking 'justification by faith' is closely tied-in to belief about Jesus' death on the cross. The teaching of Paul is that Jesus' death somehow makes satisfaction before God for the sins of others. And that is why God can accept sinners without demanding punishment for their sin. But how this comes about has been a matter of dispute between Christians. Was Jesus' death a sacrifice, like the sin-offerings in the religion of the Jews in what Christians call the Old Testament? But how did that make the difference for God? Did Jesus somehow become a substitute for others in his death, so that he took their place and received their punishment? Or is that falling back into the danger of applying the law court metaphor too rigidly? And was the effect of his death once for all, or was the sacrifice of his death somehow repeated in the mass on Sunday? This last was a matter of sore dispute between Roman Catholics and Protestants for several centuries.

There is also the question of whether God in justifying individuals *makes* them just or righteous, or merely *counts* them as righteous. This too was an issue which split Roman Catholics and Protestants for centuries following the Reformation. Catholics insisted that God's act of acceptance must make some actual difference in the life of the individual (*grace infused*), otherwise the gospel becomes a sham. Protestants were fearful that such a teaching would result inevitably in individuals once again claiming some merit for their goodness before God. Justification means grace *imputed*, otherwise the very basis of the gospel was once again under threat from human manipulation and pride.

Fortunately such disputes have been largely overcome, with each side recognizing the importance of the emphasis made by the other. Important as they are, we need not go into them further here. If readers so desire they can pursue them further in the reading suggested at the end.

More important for the theme of this book is the other main aspect of Luther's rediscovery and restatement of Paul's teaching on justification and the sequence of ideas associated with it. This whole sequence starts with and focusses in the other part of the phrase which sums up Luther's discovery – justification by *faith*. What is faith? Faith is what we described above as the sinner's 'empty hand' stretched out to receive the undeserved grace of God. As Luther realized, the classic Christian description of faith is provided by Paul in the same letter to the Romans, chapter 4. There Paul describes Abraham as *the* example of faith. And what was this faith? It was simply Abraham's trust in God's promise. Paul draws out this significance by explaining the significance of the account in Genesis – especially Genesis 15:6: 'Abraham believed God and it was reckoned to him as righteousness.'

The Genesis narrative made it all abundantly clear. God had promised that Abraham would have a son. The promise seemed wholly unrealistic, since both Abraham and his wife Sarah were long past the age of parenthood (the one about 100 years old, the other about 90). Nevertheless, the text of Genesis states that

Abraham believed the promise, and that it was by virtue of this belief that God 'took him into partnership' (this is the imagery Genesis uses).

Faith, then, is not something one does; it is not a matter of human strength or human ability. The thing that had been promised was humanly impossible. Such a promise deserved nothing more, on a human scale of values, than mockery and derision. But Abraham took God at his word; he looked not to the human situation (of his wife and himself), but relied solely on God (Romans 4:18–22). And God was able to work through that faith, through the relation of trust which his promise had made possible for Abraham, and thus to fulfil his promise in the birth of Isaac.

Luther also noted that Paul's exposition of faith was set in sharp contrast to 'works of the law'. This was the first link in the sequence of ideas building up to the complete Reformation understanding of 'justification by faith'. By 'works of the law' Luther understood Paul to mean the hard work and achievements by which one might hope to commend oneself to God. The imagery used by Paul in the same chapter contrasted 'justification by faith' with payment made for services rendered, with the wages which the worker could expect as reward for his hard work (Romans 4:4–5). In other words, 'justification by faith' has nothing to do with human achievement; it is the very opposite of earning God's acceptance.

It was this revelation which had brought such relief to Luther. For he at once realized that this is what he had been doing all along. By his penance and works of self-discipline he had been trying to commend himself to God, to build up credit with God. But no one can ever make himself or herself good enough for God. The very idea is absurd. Such perfection is beyond all human capacity. The only realistic hope of being acceptable to God is if he 'justifies the ungodly'

(Romans 4:5) – that is, if he accepts the sinner *while still a sinner*. Faith is simply the acceptance of God's offer to accept us as we are. Faith is the opposite of all human striving, and not least, the striving of religious people to prove their religious worth before God!

This application of Paul's contrast between 'faith', and 'works' to Luther's own situation as a devout but conscience-smitten monk, was, in effect, the second link in the development of the Protestant doctrine of justification. The application of language forged in the controversies of first century Christianity to the situation of a sixteenth century individual was to have major consequences for the doctrine.

But Luther applied Paul's teaching not only to himself. Paul's contrast between faith and works he saw as directly applicable to the mediaeval church as a whole. This we might say is the next link in the sequence of ideas involved in 'justification by faith'. For Luther realized that he had been misled by the teaching of the church of his time, particularly its teaching on indulgences. This was the belief, promoted from the Vatican, that the saints had built up a surplus of merit with God. This treasury of surplus merit could be drawn on, particularly by the Pope. An 'indulgence' was the name given to such a transfer of credit from the treasury of merit to an individual. Such an indulgence ensured remission of time spent by the sinful Christian in purgatory, and might even serve to remit punishment for sin entirely.

The point was, that such indulgences might be earned by diligent penance, particularly by a pilgrimage to Rome – for example, by climbing the steps of the Holy Stairs on one's knees (a practice still followed by many devout Catholics today). Or indeed, they could be earned by making a financial contribution (as a mark of contrition and confession) to the Church. This Luther now saw as the attempt to gain salvation by works. The works themselves might be good works – acts of piety and contrition – just like his own acts of penance prior to his great discovery. But Luther now saw such teaching to be wholly opposed to the teaching of Paul. Acceptability to God did not depend on good works, but could be received only by the empty hand of faith. Justification was by faith *alone* and *not* by works.

All this, as we have already said, still resonates strongly and speaks powerfully to the self-indulgent and self-righteous of the twentieth century. But it was at this point that Luther's line of thinking began to go astray – and so also the Protestant doctrine of justification which stemmed from Luther. For in spelling out his new insight into justification by faith, Luther made two assumptions, both of which can now be seen to be mistaken in some degree.

First, Luther assumed that Paul, his beloved Paul, was writing about the same experience which Luther himself had undergone. He assumed that Paul too must have gone through the same agonies of conscience about his sinfulness and inability to satisfy God which had racked Luther for so long. He assumed that Paul too must have discovered the same liberating truth of justification by faith, that Paul came to regard his previous way of life (as a pious Jew) as the way of good works. And so, for four centuries, a typical Protestant exposition of Paul's conversion would speak of Paul's troubled conscience, and of the peace with God which came to him on the road to Damascus. Typical too was the reading of Romans 7 as Paul's self-confession before he met the risen Christ – 'The good that I would, I do not; and the evil that I would not, I do . . . Wretched man that I am! Who will deliver me from this body of death?'

The trouble with all this is that when Paul speaks explicitly of his own experience before he became a Christian there is nothing of all this. On the contrary, in

Galatians 1:13–14 he speaks with the echo of his earlier pride of his success as a practising Pharisee – 'I advanced in Judaism beyond many of my own contemporaries, so exceedingly zealous was I'. In Philippians 3:6 he states quite simply that prior to his conversion he regarded himself as 'blameless as regards righteousness within the law'. In other words, there is no indication or hint of a period of guilt-ridden anxiety, like that suffered by Luther. This Protestant reading of Paul was a reading *back* of Luther's own experience *into* Paul. It was a retrojection back into Paul's first-century self-testimony of what Krister Stendahl has called 'the introspective conscience of the West'.

At this point the classical Protestant exposition of justification by faith has begun to miss the way as an exposition of Paul's teaching on the subject.

The second assumption Luther made was that the Judaism of Paul's time was just like the mediaeval Catholicism of Luther's day, at least so far as the teaching about God's justice and justification were concerned. The second assumption was natural, given the first. If Paul had made the same discovery of faith as Luther, then he must also have been reacting against the same misunderstanding as Luther. That is to say, the Judaism of Paul's day must have taught justification by works in a way wholly analogous to the teaching of the mediaeval Church about merit and the earning of or paying for indulgences.

And so, for centuries, the Judaism of Paul's day has been characterized as the prime example of a narrow legalistic religion. In particular the Pharisees, among whom Paul had numbered himself, have been depicted in countless Christian textbooks and sermons as narrow-minded, kill-joy bigots, who counted up their good works and reckoned on such to secure their eternal salvation, and who found the simple gospel of Jesus and Paul, that acceptability to God is a matter only of faith on the human side, an unacceptable affront to Judaism and worthy of death.

The trouble is that this depiction of Judaism made no sense to those Jews who bothered themselves with this Christian doctrine. The Judaism they knew emphasized human repentance and divine forgiveness – language which Paul rarely uses. When we ourselves read the scriptures of Judaism (what we call the Old Testament) the same point becomes clear. Judaism was based, after all, on the fundamental recognition that God had chosen and redeemed the people of Israel when they had absolutely nothing to commend them – when in fact they were merely slaves in Egypt. God's choice of pure grace is at the basis and heart of Jewish religion. Consider, for example, how the ten commandments begin in Exodus 20. Before laying down the law God reminds his people: 'I am the Lord your God, who brought you out of the land of Egypt, out of the house of slavery.' In other words, grace comes before law. Obedience is called for as a response to that grace, not as a way to win that grace – a very Protestant doctrine.

Nor did God require a sinless perfection from his people or require that his forgiveness had to be earned. The whole sacrificial system, including the sin-offering and Day of Atonement, was provided by God as a means of conveying forgiveness to the penitent. Consider, for example, the repeated words in the instructions regarding the sin offering in Leviticus 4:5: 'The priest shall make atonement for him for the sin which he has committed, and he shall be forgiven.' Paul's understanding of the effectiveness of Jesus' death is based directly on such a theology of sin offering.

Indeed, Paul's whole understanding of God's justice as fundamentally an act of gracious generosity is derived directly from the Old Testament, particularly the Psalms and Isaiah. There already we find an understanding of God's righteousness *not* in terms of just punishment, but rather as God's self-accepted obligation to save those who trust him despite their folly (e.g. Psalms 31:1; 35:24; 71:15; 143:11; Isaiah 51:5, 6, 8; 62:1–2). It was not Luther, or even Paul who first made the discovery about God's justice and justification, but the great spiritual writers of the Old Testament.

Here then we have something of a paradox. Luther's great discovery of justification by faith was a powerful word of God for the time. It was rooted in the teaching of Paul, and it still speaks with tremendous force to a self-centred individualism today. But it also involved a somewhat distorted reading of Paul's own self-testimony and of the Judaism within which Paul grew up. What then was it that Luther was missing? This is the question we must pursue in chapter 2.

CHAPTER TWO

Justice for Gentiles: Paul and Justification by Faith

We have seen how Luther read back his own experience into that of Paul. We have seen how Paul's experience and Paul's protest against the Judaism of his own day was understood in the light of Luther's experience and protest. But we have also noted that Luther's reading of Paul was to some extent a misreading of Paul. Paul did not share Luther's experience of an unquiet conscience before his conversion. And Paul's teaching of God's generosity in accepting the sinner by grace was thoroughly Jewish in character. Can we correct or improve that reading? What consequences might a clearer insight into what Paul meant by justification and the justice of God have for a fresh theological appraisal of twentieth century political trends?

Having moved forward in time from Luther, let us now try to move back behind Luther to Paul himself, from Paul as he was understood in the sixteenth century to the Paul of the first century itself. To understand this Paul we will have to fill in something at least of the background from which he came. To understand Paul's protest we must understand what it was that he protested against. If it was not legalistic 'justification by good works', then what as it?

The Jews of Paul's day took several things for granted (and that, of course, includes Jesus and Paul). One of these was that God is one. Each day a religious Jew would recite the Shema: 'Hear O Israel: the Lord our God, the Lord is one' (Deuteronomy 6:4). Jesus, it will be recalled, voices this confession in reply to the question, 'Which commandment is the first of all?' (Mark 12:28–29). And Paul makes the confession himself with no less vigour: 'God is one' (Romans 3:30); 'For us there is one God' (1 Corinthians 8:6); 'One God and Father of us all' (Ephesians 4:6).

Another fundamental 'given' for Jews of Paul's day was that Israel had been chosen by God as his special people. Deuteronomy gives this classic expression:

> For you are a people holy to the Lord your God; the Lord your God has chosen you out of all the peoples on earth to be his people, his treasured possession (7:6).
>
> When the Most High apportioned the nations,
> when he divided humankind,
> he fixed the boundaries of the peoples
> according to the number of the gods;
> the Lord's own portion was his people,
> Jacob his allotted share (32:8–9).

This 'theology of election' is a theme which is constantly repeated in the Jewish scriptures (the Old Testament) and in the Jewish writings of the time of Jesus and Paul.

The almost inevitable consequence was that Jews thought of themselves as different from the other peoples of the ancient world – Israel, set apart to be a people holy unto the Lord. This is a natural tendency among all nations and races. The Greeks divided the world into Greeks and Barbarians – 'us' and the rest.

So the Jews tended to divide the world into Jews and Gentiles, or Jews and Greeks (since Greek was the international language and culture of the Mediterranean world at that time).

The trouble was that Israel's theology of election gave this sense of national and cultural distinctiveness a religious dimension too. Israel had been chosen by God for himself. The other nations he had given an inferior status, having put them under the authority of other gods or angelic beings. But Israel the one God had kept for himself.

This distinctiveness was marked out most clearly by the law, the Torah – that is, the law given through Moses (making up the first five books of the Bible). In Jewish self-understanding the law had been given by God as part of his choice of Israel. In choosing Israel to be his own, God had made a 'covenant', or, we might say, a contract with Israel. Their part of the 'deal' was that they should live in accordance with the rules provided by Moses. God had promised, freely and without compulsion, to be their God – that is, to watch over them as their very own 'guardian angel', as a shepherd tends his flock. In return, Israel should live in the way that was appropriate to a people whose God was the Lord. And that way was marked out by the Torah, the law.

Here again Deuteronomy is the classic expression of this Jewish theological 'given'. The whole structure of the book gives it the character of a fundamental statement of the covenant (agreement) between God and his people. It starts in chapter 5 with the ten commandments, and climaxes in chapters 27 and 28 with the statement of the curses which would follow disobedience and the blessings which would follow obedience. If Israel needed guidance on how to 'walk' as God's people, this was where they needed to look.

Note again, in parenthesis, the undermining of any

assumption that Jewish theology taught the need to earn God's favour by doing good works. Obedience to the law, for any one who took Deuteronomy seriously, was not a way of winning God's acceptance. On the contrary, God's acceptance was the starting point of obedience. Obedience to the law was basically the response of gratitude for God's choice of Israel and covenant with Israel. In the terms laid down in Deuteronomy, one did not obey in order to enter the covenant. One obeyed because one was already in the covenant, part of the covenant people. Surprise! Surprise! Classic Jewish teaching here is very like classic Reformation teaching: that good works are the outworking of God's acceptance not the cause of it, the fruit and not the root.

But to return to our brief exposition of Jewish self-understanding at the time of Jesus and Paul. Israel's sense of distinctiveness from other nations thus had two aspects to it which become important if we are to understand what it was that Paul began to protest against.

One was the sense that the law was a kind of defensive barricade which surrounded Israel and protected it from the defilement of the other nations. God had separated Israel from the other nations, and the law preserved that separateness. This was why, for example, circumcision was so important for most Jews. As the Roman historian, Tacitus, put it: 'They adopted circumcision to distinguish themselves from other peoples by this difference.' This was why the distinction between clean and unclean foods was so important; it reinforced the difference between Israel and the nations (see e.g. Leviticus 20:24–26). Again, this was why Gentiles were forbidden to enter the Temple sanctuary in Jerusalem; Mount Zion was the focal point of God's dwelling on earth, and so the most holy of all places.

The Letter of Aristeas, a Jewish document written probably a hundred years or so before Jesus, gives a clear expression to this attitude.

> In his wisdom the legislator (Moses) . . . surrounded us with unbroken palisades and iron walls to prevent our mixing with any of the other peoples in any matter. . . . So, to prevent our being perverted by contact with others or by mixing with bad influences, he hedged us in on all sides with strict observances connected with meat and drink and touch and hearing and sight, after the manner of the Law (139–142).

In other words, the law reinforced Israel's sense of distinctiveness and separateness. To be 'within the law' or 'under the law' was to live out one's life within the terms laid down by the law, under the law's protection, as provided by God for his people.

The other aspect of Jewish thinking on election and the law was the direct corollary of the first. For if the law marked out Israel, its distinctiveness and privilege, then the Gentiles were outside the realm of that grace and favour. God might still be concerned for them, in appointing them their own guardian angels. But in relative terms the other nations were tremendously disadvantaged. The epistle to the Ephesians expresses the attitude clearly enough.

> Remember that at one time you Gentiles by birth . . . were at that time . . . aliens from the commonwealth of Israel, and strangers to the covenants of promise, having no hope and without God in the world (2:11–12).

Moreover, to be outside God's chosen people was to be outside the law. And to be outside the law was to be, in an all too real sense, an 'outlaw', a 'lawless' person, a 'sinner'. So we find, quite often, in Jewish writings of the period prior to Jesus and Paul the straight identification: Gentile = sinner, one who does not know the law, or one who knowing the law does not keep it. Paul himself echoes the attitude when he recalls his confrontation with Peter in Antioch: 'We (Peter and Paul) are Jews by nature and not Gentile sinners' (Galatians 2:15). And Jesus too may have spoken in such terms: 'If you do good to those who do good to you, what credit is that to you? For even sinners do the same' (Luke 6:33; Matthew 5:47 – 'Do not even the Gentiles do the same?').

In short, a fundamental conviction for Jews of Paul's time was that God had chosen Israel to be his own, and had given Israel the law to mark Israel off from other nations. An inevitable corollary was that the other nations, the Gentiles, were outside the scope of God's full favour, and unacceptable to him because of their lawlessness. In the light of this we can begin to understand what was the Judaism within which Paul was trained, and what it meant for Saul the Jew to become Paul the Christian.

Luther was right to see Paul's conversion as a key to understanding Paul's doctrine of justification by faith. What he failed to appreciate was the character of that conversion – what Paul was converted from, and what he was converted to.

Paul tells us quite explicitly what he was converted *from*. It was from being a persecutor of the followers of Jesus. When he recalled his 'earlier life in Judaism', the first thing that came to mind was his violent persecution of the church of God (Galatians 1:13). When he recalled his conversion, it was in terms of God's grace to him as a persecutor of the church of God (1 Corinthians 15:8–9). The three accounts of Paul's conversion in Acts have at their centre the same question heard by Paul, 'Saul, Saul, why do you persecute me?' (9:4; 22:7; 26:14). And why did he persecute? Paul himself gives the answer: it was a matter of 'zeal' (Philippians 3:6).

Now the choice of that word was not accidental. Within the Judaism of Paul's day 'zeal' had a very specific sense. It meant wholehearted commitment to safeguard the privileges and prerogatives of Israel described above from any abuse or curtailment. It included, in particular, willingness to use force if necessary to maintain Israel's set-apartness from the other nations. The ideal of such zeal was Phinehas. In Numbers 25:1–1:15 Phinehas is remembered as the one who had maintained Israel's separateness by killing an Israelite who took a Midianite woman into his tent. In Ecclesiasticus 45:23–24 this action is attributed to Phinehas's zeal. And in Psalm 106:30–31 this act is 'accounted to Phinehas for righteousness'. It was Phinehas's zeal which inspired the Maccabees to armed resistance against the attempts of the Syrian overlords to eliminate Israel's distinctiveness in the 160s BC. And it was Phinehas's zeal from which the Zealots took their name, the freedom fighters who led the fight against Rome in AD 66 in defence of the Lord God's sole crown rights over Israel.

Paul evidently thought of himself as a 'zealot' in the same tradition (Galatians 13–14; Acts 22:3). He too had been willing to take up the sword in expression of such zeal. That can only mean that he had regarded the followers of Jesus as posing a serious threat to Israel's covenant status and distinctiveness. He must have seen the openness of these first Christians to receive Gentiles into their gatherings as something which broke down the protective barrier of the law and undermined Jewish set-apartness. For Jews who believed in a Jewish Messiah fully to accept Gentiles as of their own number, without requiring them to become Jews, was too much of a contradiction for the pre-Christian Paul. Such was his zeal for the Lord and zeal for the law that he was ready to persecute and 'destroy' the new movement.

Paul is equally clear on what he was converted *to*. In a word, he was converted to the Gentiles. Or, to be more precise, he was converted to the equally burning conviction that the good news of Jesus was indeed, after all, for the Gentiles.

In fact he never speaks of his conversion as a 'conversion'. For Paul it was a calling or commissioning. The train of thought already cited from Galatians 1 runs on: '. . . God . . . was pleased to reveal his Son in (or to) me, in order that I might proclaim him among the Gentiles . . .' (1:15–16). Further in 1 Corinthians 9:1–2 and 15:8–10 the appearance of Christ on the Damascus road is thought of exclusively in terms of its constituting Paul as apostle, or missionary; that is, as always in his own self-understanding, 'apostle to the Gentiles'.

In other words, Paul was converted to the gospel that he had persecuted so fiercely. Not surprisingly, it was the element in the earliest Christian movement which he had found so offensive which became top of his own personal agenda in the complete turning upside down of his 'conversion' experience. To recognize that he had been wrong to persecute his fellow (Christian) Jews for their openness to the Gentiles was to recognize also that he must now proclaim that gospel himself.

In the light of all this we can begin to see more clearly what it was that Paul the Christian Jew protested against. What he protested against as a Christian was what he had defended so vigorously as a Pharisee. This was the conviction that God's election of Israel meant Israel's maintaining its set-apartness from Gentiles; that Gentiles as Gentiles were sinners and unacceptable to God as such; that only by being or becoming a Jew, coming 'under the law', could Gentiles participate in the blessings which belonged to Israel through the covenant.

The insight which came to him was that God's

purpose in choosing Israel in the first place always had the benefit of the Gentiles in view, the blessing of all nations. This he now saw to be the meaning of the original promise to Abraham and the other patriarchs on which the whole covenant was based: 'In you (Abraham) all the families of the earth shall be blessed' (Genesis 12:3). It is this insight which lies at the heart of his exposition in Galatians 3–4 and Romans 3–4 and 9–11. To put it another way, Paul's conversion/commissioning made him see the force of Israel's commission to be 'a light to the nations, that my (God's) salvation may reach to the end of the earth' (Isaiah 49:6). This was a passage which almost certainly lay behind his own conviction that he must now help to fulfil that very role (explicitly in Acts 13:47).

This is what the doctrine of justification by faith meant for Paul. Luther was right. It was out of his conversion experience that the Pauline teaching on justification gained its distinctive character. But that distinctive character centred on the affirmation that the unconditional grace of God had Gentiles in view as much as Jews. The doctrine of justification by faith came to expression in these key letters of Paul (Galatians and Romans) as his attempt to prove that God's covenant blessings were for Gentiles as well as for Jews, that God was ready to accept Gentiles as Gentiles, without requiring them first to become Jews. The Christian doctrine of justification by faith begins as Paul's protest not as an individual sinner against a Jewish legalism, but as Paul's protest on behalf of Gentiles against Jewish exclusivism.

The difference between the traditional Reformation doctrine of justification and the emphasis we now see to have been Paul's is perhaps clearest at two points.

One is on the theme of Jewish 'boasting'. Paul criticizes this on more than one occasion. Traditionally the boasting criticized has been understood as the boasting of self-achievement. 'No one can boast before God' can, quite naturally, and quite properly, be taken to mean, 'There is no ground for boasting before God in anything we are or do.' But when the relevant passages in Paul are examined more closely it becomes evident that that was not quite Paul's point, however true it is. When Paul introduced the theme in Romans it is quite clear what he had in mind – the boasting of the (typical) 'Jew' in his privileged position before God over against the other nations (Romans 2:17, 23). When he returns to the theme at the end of Romans 3 the object is clearly to protest against such boasting: the boasting in view is the assumption that God is to all intents and purposes God of Jews only (3:27–30). And later on he criticizes his fellow Jews for seeking 'to establish their own righteousness' (Romans 10:3). Here the meaning is 'their own' and not anyone else's, that is, 'their own' as exclusively the righteousness of Jews, a righteousness which Gentiles as Gentiles could not share in.

The other is the theme of 'justification by works'. On several occasions Paul contrasts his understanding of the way God's acceptance works in practice with the more common Jewish understanding. That 'no one is justified by works of the law but only through faith' is one of Paul's most fundamental assertions (as Luther recognized). It lies at the heart of the same letters, themselves the heart of Christianity's theological inheritance from Paul, Romans and Galatians (see particularly Galatians 2:16 and Romans 3:20–30).

But what is it that Paul was hitting out against? Again the Lutheran tradition is clear on the question. 'Works of the law' denote the good deeds, the earnest efforts and strivings, by which we may hope to commend ourselves to God. To quote the prayer of the Pharisee in Jesus' famous parable, 'I fast twice a week, I give tithes of all that I get' (Luke 18:12).

Once again, however, the interpretation is slightly skewed. 'Works of the law' is now recognizable as a phrase in use at the time of Paul. We have several examples of it in the Dead Sea Scrolls. There it refers explicitly to the particular understanding and practice of the law which characterized the Qumran community. The Qumran people, it should be recalled, were Jews who had set up a monastery in the Judean desert, in order to separate themselves from the sin which they believed had corrupted the rest of Judaism. 'Works of the law' signified that practice of the law which distinguished them from other Jews. Each year the Qumran covenanter had to be examined to see that his practice of the law was in line with this distinctive Qumran interpretation.

In other words, we are back once again in the same 'us'/'them' mentality, with 'works of the law' understood as that practice of the law which distinguished and separated 'us' from 'them'. In Paul's case 'the works of the law' was the practice of the law which distinguished Jew from Gentile, which set apart the people of God, as consisting of Jews practising the law, from all other nations. This is why the phrase in Paul usually seems to have in view such practices as circumcision and food laws in particular. For it was these practices of the law, perhaps more than any others, which marked out Jews as different from Gentiles in the ancient Mediterranean world.

We can now see more clearly what Paul was getting at when he created his classic antithesis: God justifies (accepts) people through faith and not by virtue of works of the law. He was not hitting at people who thought they could earn God's goodwill by their achievements, or merit God's final acquittal on the basis of all their good deeds. That theological insight is true and of lasting importance. But it is not quite what Paul was saying. Paul's point was rather that God accepts Gentiles in the same way that he accepts any person – by grace through faith, through their openness to receive what God wishes to give them. That is to say, God accepts Gentiles as Gentiles, without requiring them to take on a Jewish life-style or change their nationality or race.

To sum up, justification by faith as Paul formulated it cannot be reduced to the experience of individual salvation as though that was all there is to it. Justification by faith is Paul's fundamental objection to the idea that God has limited his saving goodness to a particular people.

What a tragedy that this expression of the Christian gospel has been so much neglected! Had this dimension of justification by faith not been so lost sight of in the country of Martin Luther, it would have been much less easy for Nazi racialism to promote its philosophy of the master race and to embark on the genocide of the Jews fifty years ago. It is this dimension of justification by faith which has been so ignored in South Africa of recent years. A country which prides itself in its biblical heritage has failed so signally for so long to recognize how deeply its policy of apartheid offends and destroys the gospel of justification. Sadly also some expressions of contemporary Zionism have fallen into the same trap, and in the break-up of Eastern Europe in the early '90s the same distressing formula is being repeated.

Not that we should be too quick to cast the first stone, for many British missionaries in the 19th century made the same mistake. They confused Christianity with Victorian culture and Victorian values. This mistake is often sadly repeated in North America today – the confusion of Christianity with the American way of life.

Luther needed to discover justification by faith at the individual level. Just as much today we need to rediscover Paul's original teaching on the subject. God accepts all who believe and trust in him: Gentile as well as Jew, black and white, Palestinian and Israelite, central American and US citizen, Roman Catholic and Protestant, Orthodox and Muslim. But there is yet more to be said.

CHAPTER THREE

The Justice of God

There is one further dimension of our subject which we dare not forget. For this we must go back to the *Old* Testament. We have already seen the importance of going behind the traditional Reformation understanding of justification by faith to the earlier context of Paul. Now we need to go back behind Paul to the earlier language on which he drew: from Luther to Paul; from Paul to the Old Testament. Only so will we be able to gather up the various threads which together make up the pattern of divine justice as understood within the biblical traditions.

The point is, that 'righteousness', or 'justification', is a thoroughly Old Testament concept. Luther was able to give the idea of 'justification by faith' such a central place in his reformulation of the Christian message, because Paul had made so much of it in *his* original statement of what Christianity was all about. But Paul had not invented the concept or language. When Paul brought the language of righteousness/justification to the fore it was the language of the Old Testament which he was using. As we shall see, Paul was plugging into an important theme in Old Testament writings.

That also means that Paul was assuming the *teaching* of the Old Testament on that subject. Several aspects of that teaching were not in dispute. Paul had nothing new or different to say on these aspects. So he does not mention them. He takes them for granted. He assumes that the recipients of his letters, familiar as they would be with the Jewish scriptures, would recognize the wider ramifications of the theme. That is why it is not possible to read off a comprehensive doctrine of God's justice from Paul's letters alone. What was not in dispute need not be discussed. But the fact that they were not controversial (and so not written about by Paul) did not make them any the less important. It is these 'taken-for-granted' elements of our theme, assumed and so unexpressed by Paul, which we need now to investigate.

Two of them are of first importance for us. The first is to recognize that in biblical thought righteousness is relational. The second is that in the biblical thought of justice the vertical and the horizontal are inseparable.

Righteousness in relationship

The key to understanding the theme of righteousness in the Bible, together with its related ideas of justice and justification, is to recognize that we are dealing with concepts of *relationship*. To appreciate the force of this point those of us who belong to the European tradition of thought need to take a conscious step out of our traditional way of thinking about such ideas. This is because our thinking in this area has been shaped primarily by our heritage from the classical Greek and Roman period of our history. In Greco-Roman thought 'righteousness/justice' was an ideal, to which all expressions of righteousness and justice were only approximations. Righteousness/justice was an absolute ethical norm against which particular claims and duties could be measured.

On this understanding a just/righteous act or person was one that measured up well against the standard of right. Failure so to measure up to this standard involved ethical or criminal liability or guilt. 'Justice' was like a divine principle of order which had to be sustained and appeased lest disorder and anarchy prevail. Our legal system still shows the influence of such Greco-Roman thought when we say such things as, 'The demands of justice must be satisfied.'

But this is not the way Hebrew writers understood justice. In Hebrew thought righteousness is a concept of relation. In Hebrew thought righteousness is something one has precisely in one's relationships as a social being. That is to say, righteousness is not something which an individual has on his or her own, independently of anyone else – as could be the case with the Greco-Roman concept. Rather, righteousness is a matter of the responsibilities which arise out of social relationships. People are righteous when they meet the claims which others have on them by virtue of their particular relationships.

Thus, in particular, the king is righteous when he fulfils his responsibilities as king towards his people. The servant is righteous when he obeys his master. A good example is 1 Samuel 24:17, where king Saul confesses that David was more righteous than he. Why? Because David had remained faithful to his responsibility towards Saul, as subject to God's anointed ruler, whereas Saul had abused the responsibility of his superior status and power. It was the special responsibility of the judge in ancient Israel to recognize what these various obligations were within the nation and to judge accordingly (e.g. Exodus 23:7–8; Leviticus 19:15; Isaiah 5:23). In other words, righteousness and relationship were two sides of the same coin.

The same is true, and pre-eminently so, of God's relationship with his human creatures. In Hebrew thought God is righteous because, as Creator, he sustains his creation and makes it possible for his creation to thrive. Human creatures are righteous when they recognize their creaturely status, and honour and worship God as God. This is one of the points Paul alludes to briefly at the beginning of his great exposition of the Christian gospel in Romans 1:18–23.

But in Jewish thought the more important relationship which God had undertaken was that with Israel. He had chosen Israel to be his own people, out of all the nations of the earth. His righteousness here meant his faithfulness to the obligation which he had taken upon himself in so choosing Israel. This was to support and defend Israel, to save Israel even from its own failings. Israel's righteousness, in response, was to live within that relationship, to live in accordance with the terms God laid down for that relationship. These terms were set out in the law, the Torah.

Here, then, is where the tie-in between righteousness and law begins in biblical thought, a link which has caused such confusion in Christian theology. Israel's righteousness is first and foremost an expression of her relationship with God. It is not seen as a means to the achieving of that relationship, but as the living out of that relationship. It was God who took the initiative in first choosing Israel, a slave people of little consequence in the ancient near Eastern world. To those already chosen as his people he gave the law. Only after the Exodus brought about by God's power, comes the giving of the law at Mount Sinai. The human righteousness called for and provided for in the law (obligations but also means of atonement) is conceived first of all as the response to divine righteousness. The whole position is classically set out in Deuteronomy chapters 5:1 to 29:1.

Moreover, Jewish thought emphasized the priority and indispensability of God's righteousness still more strikingly. For writers like the Psalmist or the author of the second half of Isaiah were very conscious of Israel's failure to maintain its righteousness – to keep its side of the bargain with God, as we might say. So it is in these writings in particular that we find the idea of God's righteousness merging into the idea of God's salvation. They understood the obligation which God had taken upon himself to be such that God would continue to be Israel's God even when Israel was unrighteous. God would sustain his side of the relationship even when Israel failed to uphold its side. God would continue to be righteous despite Israel's unrighteousness.

Thus, as already noted in chapter 1, we find the Psalmist calling on God to deliver or vindicate him in accordance with his (God's) righteousness (31:1; 35:24; 71:2; 143:11). And modern translations regularly translate 'righteousness' in the Hebrew and Greek as 'deliverance', 'acts of salvation', 'vindication', and so on (e.g. Psalms 51:14; 65:5; 71:15; 98:2; Isaiah 46:13; 51:5–8; 62:1–2; 63:1, 7). Here precisely is where Paul got his concept of divine righteousness – God's unconditional acceptance of the sinner. The God who acquits the ungodly (Romans 4:5) is the God who delivers, saves, vindicates failing Israel. The Christian doctrine of justification arises out of the Jewish scriptural understanding of Israel's divine election. This is also why Paul could argue as strongly as he did against what he saw to be the misinterpretation of the Jewish scriptures on this point among his Jewish contemporaries (chapter 2 above).

Several important conclusions emerge from this examination of the background of Paul's teaching on divine righteousness. (1) The Jewish and early Christian understanding of God's justice put the primary emphasis on the divine initiative, on God's readiness to do for his human creatures what they could not do for themselves, on God's readiness to 'go the second mile' and more. The concept of justice is not one of an inflexible rule or norm, where failure has to be punished unyieldingly, where the law must take its course. The metaphor of human relationship is more fundamental than that of the law court. In the law court, strictly speaking, there is no place for forgiveness. But in the biblical concept of God's justice, of divine righteousness, it is the sustaining of relationship through difficult circumstances, the healing of relationships suffering fracture by human failure, which is the more basic thought.

(2) In biblical thought human righteousness is an expression of divine righteousness. Human justice should be a reflection of God's justice. That is to say, the responsibilities laid down in the law are a response to God's initiative in rescuing Israel from Egypt and giving the law to Israel. Human righteousness, strictly speaking, arises out of gratitude for God's initiative. This is also to recognize that the system of human justice is not a self-sustaining system. Because of human greed and failure it cannot be self-sustaining. Left to itself it will always break down in disorder and chaos. From the Jewish and Christian perspective the system of human justice can work only if it is seen as a reflection of God's justice. It can be sustained only by the energy of gratitude to God and as a response to his generous purpose in his dealings with humankind.

(3) The recognition that righteousness is a matter of relationship and not of the individual as an independent agent also helps resolve some of the old problems which plagued earlier discussion of justification by faith. Is God's righteousness something he has in himself (an 'attribute'), or something he gives to others (a status)? Does God simply '*count*' someone as righteous (even when that person is still unrighteous),

or does he actually *make* the person righteous? It should be clear now that these questions arise out of the Greco-Roman context which shaped the post-biblical discussion of righteousness/justification. But once we grasp the relational character of the biblical concepts we can see that these are non-questions. For God's righteousness is his acting out of the obligation which he took upon himself in creating the world and in choosing Israel to be his people. And it consists primarily in drawing human persons into the appropriate relationship with himself and in sustaining them in that relationship. In such a relationship no human partner can remain unchanged.

Horizontal and vertical

Equally fundamental to Jewish thought is the axiom that responsibility towards one's neighbour arises out of Israel's relationship with God. God had chosen Israel to be his people and had given them the law to show them how to live as his people. Within that relationship the Israelites had a two fold responsibility – towards God and towards their fellows. The point is that the two go together. One could not be just before God without being just to one's neighbour.

This is already clear in the basic statement of Israel's responsibility under the law – the ten commandments (Exodus 20:2–17; Deuteronomy 5:6–21). As is well known, the ten commandments come in two parts, or two tables. The first deals with responsibility towards God – no other gods, no idols, keeping his name and his sabbath holy. The second deals with responsibility towards others – honour father and mother, no murder, adultery, stealing, false witness, coveting. Again the point is clear: the two go together. In Jewish thought the righteous person is one who lives in accordance with *both* tables of the ten commandments. It would not be possible to be just before God by keeping only the first four commandments and ignoring the rest, just as it would be impossible to be just before God by observing the last six and ignoring the first four. Vertical righteousness is not independent of horizontal righteousness.

A good example of this interlocking character of responsibility towards God and responsibility towards one's fellows is provided by Ezekiel 18:5–9.

> If a man is righteous and does what is lawful and right – if he does not eat upon the mountains or lift up his eyes to the idols of the house of Israel, does not defile his neighbour's wife or approach a woman in her time of impurity, does not oppress any one, but restores to the debtor his pledge, commits no robbery, gives his bread to the hungry and covers the naked with a garment, does not lend at interest or take any increase, withholds his hand from iniquity, executes true justice between man and man, walks in my statutes, and is careful to observe my ordinances – he is righteous, he shall surely live, says the Lord God.

So too the vehemence with which the prophets denounced any attempt to pull apart religious and social obligation is a prominent feature within the Old Testament. Consider for example Isaiah 58:3–7.

> (Israel speaks) 'Why do we fast, but you do not see?
> Why humble ourselves, but you do not notice?'
> (God replies) Look, you serve your own interest on your fast day
> and oppress all your workers.
> Look, you fast only to quarrel and to fight
> and to strike with a wicked fist.
> Such fasting as you do today
> will not make your voice heard on high.
> Is such the fast that I choose,
> a day to humble oneself?

Is it to bow down the head like a bulrush,
 and to lie in sackcloth and ashes?
Will you call this a fast,
 a day acceptable to the Lord?
Is not this the fast that I choose:
 to loose the bonds of injustice,
 to undo the thongs of the yoke.
to let the oppressed go free,
 and to break every yoke?
Is it not to share your bread with the hungry,
 and bring the homeless poor into your house;
when you see the naked, to cover them,
 and not to hide yourself from your own kin?

Other good examples of similar prophetic indignation are Amos 5:21–24 and Micah 3. Evidently the temptation to pull apart obligation towards God from obligation towards other people was just as great in Old Testament Israel as it is today. And the prophetic response is clear. It cannot be done. Vertical and horizontal are interlocked. It is impossible to be just, acceptable before God, while at the same time being unjust towards one's neighbour.

That is precisely why it is important to see 'justification' and 'justice' as interlocking concepts and realities. In Hebrew and Greek they are derived from the same root. The separation which has been allowed to develop between our different English words – justify, righteous, justice – should never have been allowed to happen. They belong together. It is not possible to have justification without justice.

Particularly notable within the religion of Israel is the strong sense of responsibility towards the disadvantaged of society. Within the more general obligation towards the neighbour there is a special emphasis placed on obligation towards those who are unable to fend for themselves. Characteristically those in view are the widow, the orphan, the stranger and the poor. So, for example, in Zechariah 7:9–10 –

> Thus says the Lord of hosts, Render true judgments, show kindness and mercy each to one another; do not oppress the widow, the orphan, the alien, or the poor; and do not devise evil in your hearts against one another.

This concern for the disadvantaged should not be confused with a purely individualistic charity. It was enshrined in civil law, and thus formally recognized as a responsibility of society. Here we should note above all Deuteronomy 24:10–22. Not least of interest and importance is the practicality of its legislation.

> When you make your neighbour a loan of any kind, you shall not go into his house to take his pledge. . . . If the person is poor, you shall not sleep in the garment given you as the pledge. You shall give the pledge back by sunset, so that your neighbour may sleep in the cloak and bless you; and it shall be righteousness to you before the Lord your God.
>
> You shall not withhold the wages of poor and needy labourers, whether other Israelites or aliens who reside in your land in one of your towns.
>
> You shall pay them their wages daily before sunset, because they are poor and their livelihood depends on them; . . .
>
> You shall not deprive a resident alien or an orphan of justice; you shall not take a widow's garment in pledge. Remember that you were a slave in Egypt and the Lord your God redeemed you from there; therefore I command you to do this.
>
> When you reap your harvest in your field, and forget a sheaf in the field, you shall not go back to get it; it shall be left for the alien, the orphan, and the widow, so that the Lord your God may bless you in all your undertakings. When you beat your olive trees, do

> not strip what is left; it shall be for the alien, the orphan, and the widow. . . . Remember that you were a slave in the land of Egypt; therefore I am commanding you to do this.

Also significant is the familiar imagery used in both Deuteronomy and Zechariah. The poor were to be understood not simply as neighbour, but as brother (Deuteronomy 15:11; Zechariah 7:9–10). Israel's self-understanding as son to God as Father was interdependent on recognition of the fellow Israelite, and particularly the disadvantaged member of the community, as brother. Equally significant is the fact that this obligation to one's neighbour was seen to embrace not only the fellow citizen, but also the sojourner, the resident alien. 'You shall love your neighbour as yourself: I am the Lord. . . . The alien who resides with you shall be to you as the citizen among you; you shall love the alien as yourself, for you were aliens in the land of Egypt: I am the Lord your God' (Leviticus 19:18, 34).

The Old Testament emphasis on the integration and interdependence of the horizontal and the vertical in the matter of justice and justification is thus clear. So also is the importance within the righteousness called for by God of the responsibility of the God-fearing society for its weaker members, unable to cope on their own.

For their part Christians need only recall that Jesus underlined both emphases. In answer to the question, 'Which commandment is first of all?', he stressed that love of God is the first priority. But at once he coupled with that the call for love of neighbour as oneself. The two together make up the sum and substance of the law (Matthew 22:35–40). For Jesus it was impossible to separate the two, it was impossible to conceive of an acceptability before God which did not include an acted out recognition of responsibility for the neighbour. Moreover, his parable of the Good Samaritan made it clear just how extensive that responsibility could be – crossing both religious and racial lines (Luke 10:29–37). His followers must be prepared to count even the enemy as neighbour (Matthew 5:43–48).

All this is of a piece with Jesus' openness to the 'sinner', to those unacceptable in devout religious circles (Mark 2:16–17; Matthew 11:19). From here it becomes an easy step to Paul and to Paul's insistence that the gospel of justification is precisely for the 'sinner', Gentile as well as Jew. Thus we begin to see more clearly how the whole theme of justification, justice and righteousness is indeed all of a piece for Jesus and Paul as well as for their Jewish forebears.

To sum up then. The biblical understanding of justification/justice/righteousness is all of a piece. In particular, it involves two important aspects: righteousness as essentially involving relationships, arising out of relationships, expressed in relationships; and righteousness, as both horizontal and vertical, as involving responsibility to one's neighbour as part and parcel of one's responsibility towards God. Unless these two aspects of biblical thought are firmly grasped the concept of righteousness, of justification and justice, is bound to become distorted. In Hebrew and earliest Christian thought it would not be possible for someone to be righteous apart from, without reference to, that individual's responsibility to others; it would not be possible to be righteous before God while involved in unjust relationships with fellow humans. And central within this understanding of the justice looked for by God was the recognition of society's responsibility towards the disadvantaged and the concern to conform social relationships to the model of the caring family.

When talk turns to questions of justice, then, we do well to ask: Whose justice – God's or ours?

PART TWO

THREE CASE STUDIES

Introduction

So far we have been exploring the meaning of the word 'justification'. As we moved from Martin Luther back to Paul himself, and then back further still into the Old Testament, we saw that it is a word which contains a cluster of ideas. It points first and foremost to God, who in his grace and mercy takes the initiative and accepts us while we are sinners. The Christian life is not a matter of striving for God's acceptance of us; we are already offered acceptance by God – that is the start of the Christian life, not its goal. Our task is to respond to that offer and live our lives in faith, that is, trusting in God's promises. Furthermore, that offer is open to all people. There is no question of it being confined to one group to the exclusion of others; it is open to absolutely everyone inclusively.

God's justification or righteousness is therefore deeply personal. It is God acting to vindicate us when we do not deserve it, to draw us into a personal relationship with himself. Moreover, we cannot enjoy this personal relationship on an individualistic basis, in isolation from others. Our relationship as people who are justified by God is inseparable from our relationship to our neighbour. Once again, this must be inclusive. We must be concerned with the weak and the disadvantaged – those who tend to be neglected in our societies. We must be concerned to include even our enemies. The whole of the life of society comes under the scrutiny of God. We must show our love of God and neighbour not only in our dealings with this neighbour or that, but in the very structures of communities, both national and international, which have such a powerful effect on the well-being of all their members. It is woefully inadequate to suppose that justification is a private affair, only granting peace in the heart of the individual and having nothing to do with society. Justification is inseparable from justice.

It is perhaps hardly surprising that nations do not live up to the demands of the gospel. Nationalism and racialism are all too common. The excitement of 1989, when the Berlin Wall was to dismantled and communism began to collapse in Eastern Europe, has given way to dismay at the emergence of rampant nationalism and racialism. There is a proper place for national loyalty, but all too often it has overtones of superiority and exclusivism. 'Ethnic cleansing' is a dismal addition to our vocabulary, and a nightmare for the sufferers in the former Yugoslavia. The Church has an immense role to play in combating these evils. It has to defend the victims (often Muslims) and protest against all forms of discrimination.

Yet it must be said that the actions of Christians – and even whole churches – often show that they have great difficulty in grasping the meaning of justification. Here also perhaps we should not be too surprised. It is a commonplace (and only a little introspection is needed to confirm it) that though Christians are justified by God, they remain sinners, always in need of forgiveness. The battles fought by Martin Luther, by Paul, by Jesus, and by the prophets of the Old Testament imply that the Church must engage in a never-ending struggle to grasp in heart and mind the meaning of justification.

An important point here is that it is not enough to be able to state a doctrine of justification, or any other doctrine for that matter. The core of Christianity is not simply doctrine, vital though that is, but devotion and discipleship in our whole life. We are called to respond to God's acceptance of us, and that involves a lifelong struggle to become who we are called to be and to grow into a perfect relationship with God and our neighbours. Doctrines are necessary signposts along the way, though unlike signposts, they have to become part of the fabric of our lives. Each of us belongs to a certain culture at a certain point in history, and that is equally true of the Church. In the context where we are set we are called to live faithfully to God and his promises, shown supremely to us in Jesus Christ and the gospel of justification, and to live responsibly in the world. We are to worship, pray, study the Bible and Christian history. We are at the same time to read the signs of our times in the light of the gospel, and to act accordingly. And it is only as we immerse ourselves in all those facets of our Christian discipleship that we shall come to know God and the full meaning of what he has done and is doing for us.

One way in which we can be helped along our way is to hear about the experiences of other Christians, their struggles to live faithfully. There will never be simple applications from one situation to another, but we can enter imaginatively into the situations of others and so become more skilled at reading the signs of the times in our own culture. The next two chapters tell of the experience of Christians in two parts of the world in the first half of this century. In each case there were mass failures of perception and action by Christians, but the next generation has tried to learn from those failures and strengthen the hold of the Church on the meaning of justification. The two examples are Germany and Japan.

The third example is nearer home. It is a critical reflection on the Thatcher years – an attempt to read the signs of the times in the light of the gospel of justification. Mrs Thatcher's government pursued a very different set of policies from those of the consensus of the preceding years 1945–1979 and promoted a very different ethos. She herself aimed not merely at economic and political reforms, but also at renewing the soul of the nation. How did that ambition relate to justification and justice? This question is particularly important because Mrs Thatcher is a Christian, as were many Conservative MPs and ministers, and no government in recent times cared so much about the role of the Church in the affairs of the nation. Moreover, Mrs Thatcher clearly struck chords with many Christians in the country. It was estimated that in 1979 64% of Christians who voted in the general election voted for a Conservative candidate, and most of them maintained their support right up to her departure from office in late 1990. What, then, are we to think of her administration from the standpoint of justification?

CHAPTER FOUR

Germany: A Tale of Two Kingdoms

One of the great dangers of the Reformation was that it would become more and more negative towards Catholicism. A Protestant is strictly one who speaks up positively for a certain set of Christian convictions, as Luther demonstrated in his own life. He wanted to purify Catholicism, and he retained many of its beliefs and practices, much like the English King Henry VIII. But the temptation to launch attacks against Catholicism was very strong, and Luther cannot escape some of the blame for what happened after him. He was not above intemperate attacks himself. Moreover the very route by which he recovered the doctrine of justification by faith held particular dangers. Such an introspective route could easily to lead to two unhealthy developments.

The first would be an erosion of the sense of the Church as a corporate and a world-wide body. It would be all too easy to start out from the question of my individual faith, my private relationship with God, and to think of the Church as no more than an assembly of like-minded individuals in a particular locality.

Secondly, the Catholic Church had a strong sense that the corporate and institutional life of society was to be lived in conformity with the laws of God. God, it was claimed, in creating the world had built into it a moral structure, and it was the task of human beings in their social lives to shape their institutions and their laws in accordance with that divine law. Emphasis on the individual and the individual conscience could very easily obscure that sense of a divine law governing the social life of humanity.

In short, the emphasis in Protestantism on the condition of the individual soul and its relation with God could weaken the sense of the corporate nature both of the Church and of society.

Now Luther himself did have a strong sense of the Church as a corporate body. He also believed that society should be governed according to the will of God. He had sharp things to say about the practice of usury, and about the conduct of the princes of the German states. However, the very way in which he thought of the relation of the Christian faith and politics could readily undergo a dangerous development.

Luther distinguished between two kingdoms, the kingdom on God's right and the kingdom on his left. God was Lord of both kingdoms, but they were to be run on different, and indeed apparently contradictory lines. The kingdom on the right was essentially the kingdom of the Gospel, where the pure love of God was to be expressed. This kingdom came to be associated particularly with the individual Christian and the Church. In this kingdom there is the preaching of the word and the administration of the sacraments, and the conversion and sanctification of individuals in the Christian faith.

The kingdom on the left refers to the public arena. Here Luther identified various orders, or structures of life: the family and marriage, the economy, and the state. This was really Luther's version of the Catholic idea that God has set up a certain moral structure for human life in society. It was the task of the princes of Germany to rule in such a way that these orders were maintained. Luther had a very strong sense of the sinfulness of human beings. He tended to look on the state as charged by God to maintain these orders in a godless world. The state was essentially a dyke against anarchy, and the prince was not to wield the sword in vain. In the kingdom on the left the prince would provide strong, coercive government.

There was therefore a sharp contrast, perhaps even a contradiction between the world of freedom and love according to the Gospel on the right hand, and the world of coercion in the pursuit of justice on the left hand.

In Germany in the centuries after Luther we find that this distinction between the two kingdoms hardens into a separation. Christians concentrated more and more on the bible, on preaching, and on the conversion and sustaining of individual souls. The conduct of politics, an almost alien world, was left to the godly prince.

The difficulties of this position were rudely exposed in the late nineteenth and early twentieth centuries. Before that time Germany was a country of innumerable small states. Many Germans longed for national unity. But it was only under Bismarck in the late nineteenth century that this aspiration was satisfied. The British had long enjoyed national unity. Their vast empire would have been impossible without it. The Germany of Bismarck was determined to catch up with the other great powers and find an equitable place in their company. The trouble was that Bismarck's power politics were very hard to square with the Christian ethic. The theologian Friedrich Naumann solved the problem by entirely separating the two. He declared that he had ceased to judge German imperial policy by the standards of the Sermon on the Mount. But this separation was unsatisfying and unstable.

The Germans became intoxicated with the idea of 'the people'. Indeed, this became a new order alongside the other orders of Luther. Naumann wrote, 'Peoples are great corporate personalities . . . Power lies in the devotion of the individual to the greater whole, to fellow-feeling with all who travel the same road of world history. As a people we are only parts of a very slow movement. This long life from an original people to a completely matured people is evident in war more than at any other time.' Naumann was writing in 1915.

This concept of the people did not remain simply a political one. Politicians love to have the unqualified support of religion for their designs. Christians in Germany leapt to provide it. On the very day when the First World War broke out Ernst von Dryander, Chaplain to the German court, declared, 'Looking to the state which reared us, to the Fatherland wherein lie the roots of our strength, we know that we are going into battle for our culture against the uncultured, for German civilisation against barbarism, for the free German personality bound to God against the instincts of the undisciplined masses . . . and God will be with our just weapons. For German faith and German piety are intimately bound up with German civilisation.'

So the separation of the kingdoms was transformed into their unqualified alliance. Having concentrated for so long on the individual and the private practice of the faith, Christians seemed to have no criteria for putting any bounds upon the state. They simply and abjectly endorsed the war machine.

The surrender of Germany in 1918 was not therefore merely a military defeat. It threatened to be the collapse of all meaning. One German wrote, 'The German people have surrendered their inner honour and dignity, even their self-respect. The complete destruction of all moral precepts has catapulted us into ghastly depths.' German Christians were agreed that the crisis was fundamentally religious and moral. The Protestant Church therefore had to rise to a supreme challenge and be, as one put it, 'a school of work, service, reverence and love of the Fatherland.' The individualism of the past seemed too narrow, the family too limited. Yet culture and the state had been brought to collapse. Only the people had survived. The German desire for community, service and sacrifice was now poured into the concept of the people.

Events now took a very sinister turn. The German people was not merely to recover its inner honour and dignity. The movement for the restoration of the people was marked by a strong ethical dualism. Its supporters thought in terms of good and evil, light and darkness, purity and corruption. The ideas expressed by von Dryander were as powerful as ever. The German people stood on the side of good and light and purity, and was capable of winning the battle against the forces of evil in the world.

But where was evil and darkness and corruption embodied? What were the boundaries of this German people? The finger was pointed at the Jew. Some believed that traditional racialist ideas had been scientifically proved. 'The people is an entity created by blood', wrote Max Gerstenhauer in 1920. The Jew would be the scapegoat for the loss of the war. 'Over millions of corpses surrounded by streams of blood the universal Jew strides towards the throne of world domination,' declared Theodor Fritsch. It was not long before one Adolf Hitler wrote, 'There is no making pacts with Jews. There can only be the hard either-or. I for my part decided to go into politics.'

For Hitler the unity of the German people was of paramount importance. The divisive rivalry of

Catholicism and Protestantism had to be laid to rest and both subordinated to it. That unity, Hitler proclaimed, would be essentially Christian. He assured Germans, 'We tolerate no one in our ranks who offends against the ideas of Christianity. This our movement is in fact Christian. We are filled with a desire for Catholics and Protestants to discover one another in the deep distress of our people.' And then ominously, 'We shall suppress any attempt to put religious issues on the agenda of our movement.' Clearly it was Hitler who was going to determine the content of the Christian faith. On becoming Chancellor in 1933 he declared, 'The national government will consider as its supreme and first task that of restoring a spirit of unity and purpose among our people. It will preserve and defend the foundations upon which the power of our nation depends. It will take Christianity under its firm protection, as the basis of our entire morality, and the family as the cell in the body of our people and state.'

In that year Hitler both obliged and outwitted the Catholic Church by signing a concordat with it, and vigorously promoted a German Christian Church which was to unite all Protestants under the banner of Nazism.

Once again there were lackeys among the theologians. One view in academic circles was that both Catholicism and Protestantism were distortions of the gospel, which had been foisted on the world by Paul. Theologians pointed to a true gospel behind the Jewish Paul, a pure non-Jewish gospel, which would lend support to Hitler's murderous designs against the Jews.

Moreover, paradoxically, alongside this fusion of religion and politics, there still existed the idea of the separation of the two kingdoms. Wilhelm Stapel wrote in 1933, 'The totalitarian state controls all law, all morality. The Church has all that concerns the Kingdom of heaven. Law and order in the Church are subordinate to the state. What must be conceded to the Church is that its members should be able to gather undisturbed in the name of Jesus Christ, that the Gospel should be properly preached and the sacraments correctly administered.' Clearly the Church had no voice in politics, indeed scarcely any in the organization of its own life.

By now Lutherans were so accustomed to this way of thinking and so mesmerized by the manipulations of Hitler and cowed by his terror, that they could offer scarcely any resistance. In April 1933 came the law which excluded from their posts all officials who were not of Aryan extraction. Since ministers of the Lutheran Church were also state officials, this meant that any ordained Jewish Christian was also excluded. Indeed all baptized Jews were liable to exclusion from the Christian Church. Friedrich Wieneke obligingly declared, 'The Church has to conform to the natural conditions established by God in his creation . . . Only truly German Christians belong to this fellowship. That includes every fellow member of the People with German blood . . . The baptised Jew does not belong to it.'

The acute difficulty which German Protestants had in breaking out of this impasse is very clear in the wrestlings of Dietrich Bonhoeffer. In 1933 he wrote, 'Without doubt the Church of the Reformation has no right to address the state directly in its specifically political actions. It has neither to praise nor censure the laws of the state, but must rather affirm the state to be God's order of preservation in a godless world . . . The action of the state remains free from the Church's intervention . . . Thus even today in the Jewish question it cannot address the state directly and demand of it some definite action of a different nature.'

Yet Bonhoeffer clearly could not find any peace of mind in this traditional position, for in the very same essay he declared that the state has its own responsibilities and its own boundaries. The state can be challenged if it does too little and fails to fulfil those responsibilities, or if it does too much and oversteps the bounds of its own competence. In the case of the Jews the state failed to accord to them the treatment to which they were entitled as human beings resident within the German state. The Church then had a task of aiding the victims of state action. It had an unconditional obligation to the victims of any ordering of society, even if they did not belong to the Christian community. The Church could even contemplate direct political action, as he put it, not to bind the victims under the wheel but to put a spoke in the wheel.

In 1934 the newly formed Confessing Church, led by Karl Barth and Martin Niemoeller, issued the Barmen Declaration. This defended the integrity of the Christian gospel and Church against the attempts of Hitler to corrupt them from within by setting up the German Christian Church. Bonhoeffer was not at Barmen, but he quickly became a leading figure. Indeed he sometimes dismayed the Confessing Church by the strength of his stand. He insisted that the German Christian Church was no Church, because it had allowed the corruption of the gospel, and that the Confessing Church was the true Church. He became one of the very few, even within the Confessing Church, to challenge the state on the issue of the non-Christian Jews. And finally he was led to the conclusion, deeply agonizing for one reared as a Lutheran, that the extremity of the situation warranted an attempt to assassinate Hitler. For this he was ultimately to pay with his life.

Since the Second World War Lutherans have made enormous efforts to learn the lessons of the late nineteenth and early twentieth centuries. What precisely went wrong? Surely if the Lutheran Church failed so miserably to offer any challenge to Hitler over the extermination of millions of Jews, then something was drastically wrong with its theology, with its understanding of the Christian faith and the relation of that faith to society. The well-nigh exclusive emphasis on individuals and their relationship to God had left the Lutheran Church virtually naked in its dealings with the public realm. As a consequence it had found itself assimilated to the Nazi ideology and (with a few notable exceptions) offering uncritical endorsement. Lutherans have felt the acute need to go back into their tradition, back to Luther, back to the Bible, in order to acquire a deeper hold on their faith, so that they will never again fail to read the signs of the times and to speak out against racial discrimination and genocide, or indeed any evil of similar magnitude.

Two styles of thought have been evident. The first has claimed that the Lutheranism of the Nazi period was a distortion of the teaching of Luther. Luther did not separate the two kingdoms, and there is a strong connection in his thinking between the private and the public realms. Lutherans can therefore harmonize their own tradition, at its best, with the insights of Barmen: Christians must defend the integrity of the Church and ask critical questions about the role and limits of the state. They are to live by the Pauline injunction: 'Do not be conformed to this world but be transformed by the renewal of your mind.' (Rom. 12:2) This is as valid in politics as it is in the Church.

Others despair of the model of the Two Kingdoms and prefer to work in the style of Barmen itself. Each of the theses of the Barmen Declaration offers a biblical text, a one-sentence commentary, and then a direct inference to the situation of 1934. Thus, since God made Jesus Christ our wisdom, our righteousness and sanctification and redemption (I Cor.1:30), then God is our only sovereign Lord, and we must reject the false idea that there are other lords who have a final claim on us in addition to God.

Perhaps the best known German theologian to have wrestled with these problems is Ulrich Duchrow. Twenty years ago he published a massive volume which investigated the roots of the doctrine of the Two Kingdoms, tracing them back to the Bible. He then turned his mind to the question of how that doctrine could be purged of its distortions and made serviceable again. He believed that Luther's insights were fundamentally right. The doctrine of the Two Kingdoms encapsulates the basic movement of scripture, that there is an eschatological battle being played out between the kingdom of God and the kingdom of evil, and that Christians live as members of both kingdoms, since they are justified by God's grace through faith, yet remain sinners and deny their calling. Christians have therefore to struggle both in themselves and in the world to be faithful disciples. In their own lives they must always be seeking the forgiving grace of God anew. In the world they must learn to recognize the powers of evil for what they are and fight against them. In order to do this Duchrow believes that Christians must use all the sources of wisdom available: the bible, the Christian tradition (and especially the Reformers), ecumenical reflection, contemporary experience (especially where the Church has had to face actual menace and resist, as in the 1930s), and other disciplines which throw light on our world, and particularly on the enormous concentrations of power which are exercised by the few over against the many.

In recent years Duchrow has been a strong supporter of the voices of protest coming from the Third World against the capitalist system, and 500 years on from Columbus' landing in the Americas he is pressing Europe to recognize the immense exploitation which it has perpetrated on the rest of the world and to find a better system. He himself looks on capitalism as centrally about the uncontrolled accumulation of money at the expense of the poor and powerless, and therefore to be repudiated by the Church in the same way as Nazism was at Barmen in 1934.

Many would not agree with Duchrow's conclusions, but the main point is that he and other German theologians have struggled against the reduction of the doctrine of justification to individual piety, in order to arrive at a deeper understanding of the relation of justification and justice which is theologically sound and so provides basic guidelines for faithful Christian living amid the enormous issues of our modern world.

CHAPTER FIVE

Japan: Imperial Missions

Nazi racialism is perhaps the most flagrant denial of the doctrine of justification by faith. It excluded Jews not only from the state, but even from the Church, as if God's saving goodness were valid only for Aryan Christians. The system of apartheid in South Africa has offended against the gospel of justification almost as deeply, since it has treated the Afrikaner as specially chosen by God, and thereby stamped black African experience of culture and religion as inferior.

Most Britons have long castigated such examples of racialism, but if we care to listen, we know that the British themselves in the nineteenth and early twentieth centuries had a sublime confidence in the superiority of their own culture. It did have its laudable standards. For example, Edmund Burke, the eminent eighteenth-century Whig, impeached Warren Hastings for maladministration in India. However, Burke never supposed that the Indians had the right not to be ruled by the British at all. And the British thought nothing of imposing their own cultural preferences upon indigenous peoples; indeed, they called it 'the white man's burden'.

Moreover British missionaries were heavily implicated in British imperialism. They had no doubts about the superiority of British culture and their own brand of Christianity. The two were fused. A good example, which became much clearer during the Australian centenary celebrations in 1988, is the British treatment of aborigines. An entirely negative view was taken of their culture. Aborigines were treated as if they were only sub-human, and their children were forcibly taken away to be educated according to the canons of Western culture and Western religion.

Less well-known is the history of Japanese Christianity over the last 125 years. Here we find a double example of the boastful sense of superiority, British and Japanese. It also links well with the problem of individualism and the relation of Christianity to politics which we encountered in twentieth-century Germany.

Catholic missionaries had arrived in Japan in the middle of the sixteenth century and had been quite successful in winning converts. However, in 1587 a new shogunate, the Tokugawan, began to establish central control from Tokyo over the whole country. Christianity was perceived as a threat to the new social order. The missionaries were banned from Japan, and soon the converts were persecuted almost to the point of extinction. Moreover, no Japanese was allowed to travel abroad on pain of death, and Japan entered two and a half centuries of self-imposed isolation.

In 1868 the ailing Tokugawan shogunate was finally replaced by a group who wanted radical change. They brought the 15-year-old Emperor Meiji to Tokyo from the old capital, Kyoto. For centuries the imperial duties had been mainly the ceremonies of Shinto, the native religion of Japan. Meiji was to have a stronger role as head of the new state.

These new rulers were alarmed by the strength of the Western imperial powers in Asia and their own comparative weakness, and were determined not to go the way of India. They wanted to modernize Japan and make her into a power of the first rank. They knew they would have to imbibe Western technical knowledge in order to catch up, and they studied Western imperial techniques. They opened Japan to Western education, and once again permitted Christian missions.

The missionaries (this time largely Protestant) naturally approved of the thirst of the Meiji regime for Western technical knowledge, and responded by founding schools, hospitals and other institutions, which promoted technical learning within the context of the Christian faith. They brought many cultural benefits, but also revealed their limitations. They were confirmed in their conviction that the advanced state of education, medicine and culture in the West proved the superiority of their Christian civilization. In their churches they concentrated on personal repentance and the saving of individual souls. They stressed personal piety and discipline and the moral conduct of life. They conspicuously advocated monogamy and opposed smoking and drinking. They had their reservations about the culture of Japan. One missionary expressed indignation that Japanese men wore kimonos and sat cross-legged on the floor, thus exposing their legs. 'We must teach the Japanese,' he wrote, 'to put buttons on their kimonos and to sit in chairs rather than cross-legged on the floor.'

In the public arena they did not ask any profound questions about the emerging nature of Japanese society under Meiji. This was partly because of their understandable wish not to offend their hosts, and partly because of their blithe assumptions about the superiority of Western civilization. But it was also because they treated the Christian faith as if its remit was almost exclusively personal repentance and the saving of individual souls. This preoccupation deprived most Christians of the possibility of seeing anything problematical about what was unfolding before their eyes.

During the early Meiji years there was much debate over the proper scope and use of Western ideas, but gradually a dual policy emerged which was not easy to carry through simultaneously. The leaders wanted to avail themselves of Western knowledge, especially technical knowledge, whilst achieving an unprecedented degree of national solidarity and unity. Clearly it might be difficult to restrict Western influence to technical knowledge. Western liberal values might destroy the native Japanese ethos. It would require the strong exercise of political power within Japan to consolidate national unity. The leaders became determined that Western technical learning would serve the modernization of Japan, but entirely within the Japanese spirit. And this they assiduously promoted and harnessed in a complete ideology.

The Emperor's position had varied in Japanese history. In some periods he had been a religious figurehead with little political power. But the Meiji oligarchy bolstered his political power and brought together a number of long-standing assumptions and attitudes, fusing them together into an ideology which became a very potent instrument of imperial policy.

At the heart of this ideology was religion. Shinto is the ancient religion of the Japanese people. It sees the divine as rooted in nature and especially in the soil of Japan. Traditionally it embraced also the whole Japanese people. According to Shinto, Japan is the land of the gods, and the Emperor is both god incarnate and the father of the Japanese people.

The agents of Meiji took these elements and disseminated the doctrine of the unity of the Japanese people with their Emperor, whereby they shared in his divinity. Through a new constitution and other edicts the Meiji regime reinforced the idea of the dependence of all the Japanese on their Emperor and demanded absolute obedience. The numerous shrines across the country were taken under central control, and one shrine (Yasukuni, in Tokyo) was designated as the holy place of the nation for the veneration of war heroes.

The Meiji policy was highly successful. Above all it provided the Japanese with an immensely strong sense of their corporate identity. It put them on their guard against the threat from the West and neutralized it. Western influence was largely confined to its technical knowledge. Moreover, the technological development under Meiji led to mass migration to the cities. This carried with it the danger of a loss of identity among the migrants, since they were removed from their villages and the ancestral graves there. The nationalist ideology fostered by the Meiji regime provided a focus of continuity.

Most Christian missionaries seem to have realized few of these developments. They shared the Western view that the Emperor was largely a political figurehead, and they do not seem to have realized the essentially religious nature of the whole Emperor system, and the huge barrier it would pose to successful missionary work. One of the few exceptions was Basil Hall Chamberlain, a Christian who was professor at Tokyo Imperial University. He wrote, 'The new Japanese religion consists . . . of a belief that Japan is as far superior to the common ruck of nations as the Mikado is divinely superior to the common ruck of kings and emperors.' Many Japanese converts to Christianity came from the warrior class and held responsible positions under Meiji. The missionaries were optimistic that the patriotic fervour of the converts for building a new nation would simultaneously help the spread of the Christian faith.

They were cruelly deceived. Japanese nationalism and militarism gathered in intensity and led to a succession of wars, from the Sino-Japanese War of 1894–5 up to the Second World War. The Japanese slogan was, 'All corners of the world under one roof'. The Church was increasingly forced to co-operate with Japanese expansion. As modernization proceeded apace and Japan caught up with the West in its technical and military capacity, so the Christianity which had assumed an important role was cast aside. The technical knowledge had been imbibed, but Christianity as a religion remained alien. It was tolerated only if it was totally assimilated to the Japanese spirit and ideology. Some Japanese Christians demonstrated their allegiance by making hostile attacks on the Western churches and severing contact with them. These Christians were in much the same position as the members of the German Church who gave unquestioning allegiance to Hitler.

Most Christians offered no resistance to the Japanese ideology, and indeed most had no standpoint on which to base any resistance. Those who did resist found not only savage repression from the authorities, but even incomprehension from their fellow-Christians. They were branded as traitors and anti-nationals.

So we have a double example of that exclusivism which cuts across the Pauline gospel of justification. First, the British missionaries arrived confident in the superiority of their Christian civilization. They clearly hoped that their Christianity would be swallowed along with the whole Western ethos, down to chairs and buttons. Evidently God could not accept the Japanese as members of their own culture. Understandably the Japanese were not prepared to alienate themselves from their own cultural identity.

Secondly, those Japanese Christians who assimilated their Christianity to the Japanese ideology, either actively or passively, offended also against the gospel of justification by their exclusiveness. For they accepted the violent imposition of Japanese superiority on the peoples of East Asia and put Japanese nationalism before their membership of the world-wide Church.

Yet God's gift of justification has not failed. Since the Second World War thoughtful Christians in Japan have reflected earnestly on the failures of the past, and have tried to help in building a healthy Japanese society and relations of trust and friendship with their East Asian neighbours. The central question is, how can the gospel of justification be effectively shared with the Japanese? Here is a huge task. Christianity has been perceived by the Japanese as alien and a threat to their culture, and to this day Christians number only about one per cent of the population. Today's Japanese Christians are not deterred either by their minority status or indifference or hostility. An important conviction is that the Japanese must work out their own authentic expression of Christianity. It must take genuine root in Japanese culture. In the process it will not leave that culture unchanged; but its starting point must be Japanese culture.

One possible clue in that culture is the deep Japanese longing for identity within community. The West has thrown immense emphasis on the freedom and dignity of the individual. This has grown (though only in part) out of Christian insight. We have already noted Martin Luther's profound sense of the individual conscience and of God's offer of grace and mercy to every individual. Christians (the Confessing Church is an obvious example) have often used such insights to ward off the intrusions of the state into the lives of individuals in Church and society. The Japanese experience has been very different. Traditionally the basic unit of society has been the extended family, embracing not only living members but also the ancestors and the generations yet to be born. In spite of the huge changes in Japanese society in the last 125 years, there is still a strong sense of this wide family. What is more, the concept of the family is extended to wider groupings – the school, the company, and even the whole Japanese people. Japanese societal, economic and political life is marked by networks of personal relationships with a strong sense of mutual obligations. The Japanese are taught to cultivate sensitivity towards each other within these groups and to seek harmonious relationships. There are doubtless many defects in this system, and it does seem to most Westerners that there is a regrettable tendency for the individual to be subordinated to the expectations of the group. But the Japanese do have a deeper communitarian sense than is common in the West, and this is basically very precious.

Some Japanese Christians believe that in the past the Christian faith has been presented to the Japanese too individualistically, but that it can commend itself if it respects the deep-seated desires of the Japanese for community and presents stronger evidence of the Church as a community. Clearly, such evidence would include a profound concern for the individual within the community. It would be a question of a right balance between the individual and community elements in the Christian faith. Perhaps the Japanese Church and the Churches in the West have much to learn from each other as they seek from very different contexts and experiences to work out the implications of the gospel of justification and justice.

One clear implication of that gospel is an openness and an inclusiveness towards outsiders. It is here that Japanese Christians have taken a particularly strong lead. They are very much aware that in the period up to 1945 the Japanese developed an intense and exclusive solidarity among themselves, which expressed itself in aggressiveness towards other countries. It is also the case that there has been a longstanding tendency to treat resident minorities and migrant labourers as outsiders and to exploit them. Christians have shown a deep concern for the lowest classes of Japanese, who experience very poor conditions as day labourers (the underside of the Japanese practice of guaranteeing some workers lifelong employment). They also strongly support those Koreans who were brought over forcibly to Japan in the 1930s and 1940s to provide cheap labour, and who decided to stay there in 1945. Even their children and grandchildren, who have spent all their lives in Japan, are treated as aliens and finger-printed. Christians have also set up a refuge in Tokyo for girls from East Asia (the Philippines especially) who are enticed to Japan as entertainers and are forced into prostitution by the Japanese mafia.

Thoughtful Japanese Christians are also deeply aware of the immense injury which Japanese militarism inflicted upon the countries of East Asia in the first half of this century, and they do what they can to further the restoration of relations with Japan. They have repeatedly expressed their sense of guilt. The National Christian Council in Japan set up a Centre for Christian Response to Asian Issues, whose Director travels widely in East Asia seeking reconciliation and networks of friendship with Asian Christians. The last Director was deeply impressed with the readiness of Asian Christians to receive and welcome her, and some have made return visits to Japan, where the aim is to sensitize Japanese Christians to their wider responsibilities in East Asia. Christians are alarmed today at Japan's economic dominance over East Asia, and at its tendency to exploit the manpower and natural resources of East Asia. They help to press the case of East Asians who protest about the conditions of work in Japanese subsidiaries. Or they call in question the vast consumption of timber from East Asian forests by the Japanese, and try to extend their renowned sensitivity to nature to include environmental protection beyond their shores.

One Christian agency in Japan trains Asians for leadership in rural areas in East Asia, where they set up projects to promote economic and social viability for village communities.

In all these ways Christians in Japan are creating bonds of solidarity with other countries, thus giving expression to the gospel requirement to cross boundaries and be open and inclusive, especially towards the weak. If old fears are ever to be laid to rest in East Asia, it will be of critical importance, so many Christians believe, that Japan fully accepts her international responsibilities. This is slowly developing. But until 1945 Japan acknowledged no higher law or being than the state and the Emperor. There is no tradition of natural law or natural rights, such as was invoked at the Nuremberg trials of the Nazi war criminals. Nor does the native Japanese religion Shinto know of any being higher than the land and people of Japan. In the past the Japanese were entirely justified in fearing the ambitions of the Western powers. Without condoning Japanese aggression, we can say that the arrogant imperialism of the West in Asia was no mean factor in provoking the Second World War on its Asian front. Japanese Christians are showing the way we must go if we are to give the gospel of justification and justice expression in the international arena today.

CHAPTER SIX

Britain: Free Market and Faith

If German and Japanese Christians can write so critically about the history of their own country, then a Briton ought at least to offer some reflections about Britain, in the light of our fresh understanding of justification and its integral relation with justice.

From the end of the Second World War right up to the 1970s there was a consensus between the two major political parties on certain basic issues. The recommendations of Sir William Beveridge for the extension of welfare were largely implemented by the Attlee administration between 1945 and 1951. When the Conservatives returned to power they made no attempt to dismantle the welfare state. Many Conservatives, such as Harold Macmillan and Edward Heath, were as keen as Labour that the days of poverty and want between the two world wars should not recur. There was rather more disagreement between the two parties on the issue of nationalization, but even here Labour's programme was relatively modest, and the Conservatives were modest in their reversal of Labour policy. Coal, electricity and gas remained public utilities. It was accepted that the state had an important role to play in furthering social justice, in particular by protecting the poor and the weak.

This consensus was largely underwritten by Christians who tried to bring their faith to bear upon social questions. A Low cartoon in the Manchester Guardian depicted William Temple, their chief mentor, as quite undaunted when Colonel Blimp waved his stick at him and told him to stop trespassing on the economic fields. Temple's conviction was that every area of life was subject to the demands of God's law. His guidelines in the fields of economics and politics were the dignity and freedom of the individual, coupled with the social character of every human being, and the need for human beings to serve each other and the common good. He grounded these principles in the doctrines of creation, the incarnation, the Church as the Body of Christ, and the eternal destiny of human beings. He had died suddenly in 1944, but he would certainly have been at home in the years of the Attlee administration. Indeed, he has been described as one of the foundation piers of the welfare state.

The ideas of Temple are quite easy to detect forty years later in the report of the Archbishop of Canterbury's Commission on Urban Priority Areas, *Faith in the City*. But by then the consensus was already in ruins. It had come under severe strain through the various crises of the 1970s. The quadrupling of the price of oil, and the failure of the Labour Government of Harold Wilson to deal effectively with inflation and labour unrest called in question the competence of the state to manage the economy, industrial relations and welfare. In the middle of the 1970s the Conservative Party chose a new leader with a radically different approach to politics and economics. Six years into Mrs Thatcher's time as Prime Minister it was hardly surprising that *Faith in the City* was sharply taken to task, as it conspicuously failed to address itself to the arguments of the new approach. To go on repeating the axioms of the post-war consensus as if nothing had happened was not good enough.

It has to be frankly recognized that there is a solid body of thought lying behind the policies which have been practised in Britain since 1979. The chief guru was Friedrich von Hayek, an Austrian long resident in the US and a professional economist who worked out a whole social philosophy. According to Hayek, human beings are each a bundle of private desires, wants and goals which they seek to satisfy as far as possible. Society came into being because human beings discovered that they would achieve greater satisfaction in a social environment than outside it. They came to appreciate the value of co-operation for them as individuals and they retained successful ways of co-operating. The kind of society in which we live in the West, the Open Society, is the result of centuries of experimentation. Nobody planned our society; rather our rules of social co-operation are the unintended result of ever more successful experiments in social co-operation. In modern society there are no concrete collective goals, only these abstract procedural rules, which co-ordinate human effort in the most effective way, to satisfy individual desires.

For Hayek the individual and his wants are sovereign. 'The individual deserves respect *qua* man, and as such must be given the right to free development, power over his destiny, choice and responsibility.' Liberty is defined by Hayek as the state in which a person is not subject to coercion by the arbitrary will of another or others. Modern society has no concrete goals, nor should anyone prescribe such goals, for that would infringe human freedom and thus be a form of coercion. All that is needed are the abstract rules of social co-operation, which do not interfere with the liberty of the individual.

Hayek asks what mechanism will respect the

character of the Open Society and of the free individuals living within it, giving them the best chance of satisfying their wants. The answer is the market. The market copes with our inescapable ignorance of people's wants, whereas a central economic planner could not. The price system signals to individuals in the market place what range of wants others have and the extent to which they desire them to be satisfied. It allows producers to compare various scarcities and demands and work out the most efficient and least costly way to produce goods. Efficiency depends on an open and competitive market so that experimentation and innovation will flourish. Moreover the mechanism of the market is entirely individualistic. It has no single aim or purpose, nor is it the creation of any conscious design or planning. It is spontaneous, like society itself. It is structured and orderly, not by design but though the emergence of general rules like property and contract. Within it individuals' wants are sovereign. Individuals can frame and pursue their own ends and purposes. The value of things in the market is therefore entirely subjective.

So the accent goes on the freedom of the market and the freedom of the individual. It is important to notice that the market is not subject to any enquiry about its justice. Hayek was scornful about the pursuit of social justice, calling it a mirage. For him the justice of the market is located only in the rules for its operation. The outcomes of the market are a matter of luck, skill and judgment. It is rather like playing a game. No one would claim it was unjust to lose a game unless one's opponent had flouted the rules. It is only in this sense that the question of justice arises in the public realm of Hayek. The public realm is sharply distinguished from the private, where individuals decide for themselves on their values and their goals. One of the strengths of Hayek is that he recognizes the pluralistic and secular character of the modern world. He copes with this by minimizing the emphasis on public norms and relegating values to the private realm as subjective creations of individuals.

Hayek was not a religious man. It is, however, striking that many members of the Conservative government are practising Christians and have looked to the Church to support them. They have complained that the Church pontificates on economic and political affairs from a state of ignorance and fails to carry out its primary task, that of propagating sound doctrine and morality and the conversion of the individual to the Christian faith. Many of the insights of Hayek, it is claimed, can be accommodated without much adaptation into a Christian framework. The crux here is that the realm of economics is autonomous, and the Christian faith, it is held, is addressed essentially to individuals. Each individual is summoned by God to exercise freedom and responsibility which no one can legitimately take away. It is not only economically and politically unsound for the state to be endlessly protecting individuals. It is also morally corrupting. People become improvident and feckless, blaming everyone but themselves and making ever increasing demands upon the state, to which politicians are lamentably liable to pander.

In making these points Christians refer frequently to the parable of the talents, and to Jesus' assurances in Mark 7 that evil flows outwards from the heart. This text is used to discount the idea that human responsibility can be eroded by the circumstances in which one lives. The justification by God of the individual in his private life takes pride of place. Justice is the quality expected of an individual in his conduct in society, for example, in his respect for the freedom and rights of others or his contractual responsibilities. It is in this context that the remark of Mrs Thatcher, 'There is no such thing as society', achieves a plausibility. People cannot be justified by God *en masse*, and the health of society, it would be claimed, depends not on the pursuit of some vague notion of social justice, but on the just dealings of individuals with other members of society.

Before we leap to agree with these enthusiastic Christian supporters of the New Right, as it is called, we need to ask some hard questions from the standpoint of our understanding of justification and justice. Obviously they are not entirely wrong. They give ample space for justification by faith in the sense of the individual rejoicing at her or his acceptance by God. No one should wish to undermine individual freedom and responsibility. It is also true that earlier forms of Christian thought about society have tended to be rather dismissive of the market; yet as a way of organizing the economic life of society it has been more successful in multiplying goods than any other known method. However, there are problems.

First of all, some Christians even rejoice in the neutrality of the market place: the fact that all are bound equally by the same rules of the game and that its outcomes are simply what they are, not subject to any moral or religious critique. Yet this is difficult to square with the biblical understanding of the covenant, of a community under obligation to God and to one another. The whole of ancient Israel's life came within the scope of its relationship with its creator and redeemer, God the Father. As we have seen, the prophets raised very directly the question of the impact of certain activities in Israel upon other members of the covenant community. The content of the law was not simply a set of procedural rules but included specific directives about the treatment of the members of the community, and especially the poor. If then the market is to be accepted, it cannot be accepted for its neutrality, but because it is an instrument which best serves the good of all. In other words it would be a procedural neutrality for the sake of the common good and the good of the individuals within the community.

A major problem with the market is that within it there are very wide differences in power. Those who have resources are in a far better position to satisfy their desires than those who do not. Indeed the market will often provide luxuries for the affluent few but fail to provide for the basic needs of the poor. To say that, however, is to reinstate in the public arena some concept of what is due to human beings and to imply that it will be the function of government to make sure that basic needs are met. They will not be met, nor indeed ought they to be met, merely through charitable giving by private individuals.

There is a further difficulty which arises if the market is given too much prominence. The market is built on contractual relationships between those pursuing their interests in the market place. A constant peril is the commercialization of relationships in the public arena; that is to say, people become habituated to approaching others from the standpoint of some commercial arrangement. This peril is especially acute if a sharp division is made between the public and private arena, as if the more profound bonds between human beings can be left to the private sphere and private choice, whereas the public realm can be run on a completely different basis.

This question of bonds requires deeper exploration by considering the concept of freedom beloved of the New Right. Hayek is quite right to stress the importance of the individual as one who makes choices. Yet one must ask whether his account of human beings is adequate either on the basis of our experience of life or from a Christian point of view. We seem to start with an isolated individual who then chooses his values and chooses to relate to others. Yet surely our life is much more fundamentally relational from the very outset. We stand in a relationship to God and to other human beings which both sustains us and challenges us to respond. Surely Christian social thinkers like Temple have been right to point not simply to the freedom and dignity of each individual but also to the fact that we are inherently social. It is perfectly true that the concept of community is widely used in a nostalgic way which has little relation to the pluralistic character of the modern world. Yet the public arena must rest on more than contractual relationships. It must rest on deeper bonds, bonds which include the notion of altruism. Freedom from coercion can never be enough. Freedom must carry with it the concept of freedom for responsible action, and that must include meeting the basic needs of the poor, both physical and social.

There is a further problem with 'freedom from'. When Mrs Thatcher addressed the Church of Scotland General Assembly in 1988 she made much of freedom to choose. She seemed to think that the story of the fall in Genesis 3 illustrated this notion. Yet the story points above all to our wilful, compulsive failure to respond in gratitude to God's care for us. Those who think like Mrs Thatcher seem to envisage individuals standing before two possibilities, good and evil, with perfect freedom to choose which path they will take. Yet to construe the matter this way is to undercut the very intelligibility of the notion of justification. The doctrine of original sin in no way undermines personal responsibility, but it does point to our deep entanglement in failure to obey God, which in turn leads us to cast ourselves on his mercy. The authentic note is captured in the hymn, 'Just as I am, without one plea', not in 'Just as I am, young, strong and free'.

This particular point is of considerable importance because it is inseparable from the very style which was adopted by the Conservative government under the leadership of Mrs Thatcher. It was a highly confrontational style which has tended to divide people into 'us' and 'them'. Those who shared Mrs Thatcher's philosophy could pass muster as 'us'. The rest remained 'them'. This trait was reinforced by Mrs Thatcher's tendency, even in highly complex and ambiguous situations, to believe there is one absolutely right choice to be made. This is well documented, for example, in Hugo Young's biography of Mrs Thatcher, *One of Us*. If there is a simple choice between two paths, good and evil, then one's opponents are guilty of manifest moral obloquy. It is no surprise that dissenters from Mrs Thatcher were the recipients of self-righteous contempt (the issue of sanctions against South Africa is a good example). How this can be reconciled with our understanding of justification and justice it is impossible to see.

A consequence of this outlook is that everyone is encouraged to look with fear on those who appear to be different, and to erect protective barriers to keep them at bay. It is particularly the poor in this country who have suffered from this form of exclusion. No attempt is made to see life from their standpoint or to show any empathy with them. So far from seeing the poor as brothers and sisters in the same community, they are treated as aliens, scarcely worthy of citizenship until their souls are conscripted to the prevailing dogmas.

What we have to do with here is a kind of spirituality which is far removed from any notions of justification and justice. At its worst it is a hard morality of individual effort. It has certain points of contact with the Christian faith, but those points are ripped out of context and made to subserve an ideology. The missing context is that to which the concepts of justification and justice point: God's initiative in graciously entering into a covenant relationship with us, a relationship which is offered to all, whatever their class, nation or race; God's offer of mercy and forgiveness which sustains the covenant even in the face of human failure and sin; God's special concern that the poor and the disadvantaged should be treated with just as much respect and care as the other members of the community.

To say this is not to advocate a simple return to the post-war consensus or to the Christian social ethics which supported it. There can be no going back, only a going forward. Unlike the last two chapters, this one is not focussing on events of fifty years ago and asking what Christian responses there have been since. This history has yet to be made. And we all have a responsibility for making it, in the light of the gospel of justification and justice.

Conclusion

Here then is a message which surely needs to be heard more widely and more clearly. Justification with God and justice between nations and individuals belong inextricably together. For demonic powers seek to force us into renewed forms of narrow nationalism and racialism, where 'ethnic cleansing' becomes a conceivable and even acceptable policy option. And renewed forces of materialism are trying to keep justice and justification apart – to privatize religion and leave justice to the mercy of the market place. Under this philosophy justification by faith can mean simply the individual's finding peace with God, and the rest left to market forces.

But we cannot! We dare not! If we want our gospel and our faith to be properly rooted in the Bible, if we want our faith to be the faith of prophet and of Paul, the faith Jesus called for, then we dare not forget all three dimensions of justification by faith.

Justification by faith means not simply the individual rejoicing at his or her acceptance by God – basic and fundamental as that is. It means also recognition that justification stands opposed to any and every nationalistic or racialist narrowing of God's grace. It means also recognition that justification without justice to neighbour and poor is a contradiction in terms. To attempt to maintain such a separation of justification and justice is a fundamental perversion of biblical religion and Christian faith. What God has joined let not man put asunder!

Questions for Discussion

1. a) How would you define 'justice'?
b) Is 'justification' still a meaningful term today? What would you replace it with?

2. If the opposite of 'justification by faith' for Paul was 'justification by works', what is the opposite of 'justification by faith' today?

3. Is the spirit of nationalism a healthy or unhealthy expression of nationhood? What are its strengths and dangers? How can the dangers be countered?

4. To what extent can the Church tell the State what to do? To what extent can and should the social obligations laid down in Deuteronomy and fought for by the prophets apply in the very different societies of today?

5. What can Britons today learn from the experience of Germany and Japan earlier this century, allowing for the differences of time and culture?

6. In what directions should we try to shape the future of Britain into the twenty-first century in the light of the gospel of justification and justice?

Suggestions for Further Reading

Biblical and historical background:

E.R. & P.J. Achtemeier, 'Righteousness', *Interpreter's Dictionary of the Bible*, ed. G.A. Buttrick (Nashville: Abingdon, 1962) Vol. 4 pp. 80–5, 91–9

J.D.G. Dunn, *Jesus, Paul and the Law: Studies in Mark and Galatians* (London: SPCK, 1990)

D. Field, ed., *Here We Stand: Justification by Faith Today* (London: Hodder & Stoughton, 1986)

H. Küng, *Justification. The Doctrine of Karl Barth and a Catholic Reflection (London: Burns & Oates, 1981)*

A. McGrath, Iustitia Dei: A History of the Christian Doctrine of Justification (Cambridge University, 1986) 2 vols

A. McGrath, *Justification by Faith* (Grand Rapids: Zondervan, 1988)

J. Reumann, *Righteousness in the New Testament* (Philadelphia: Fortress, 1982)

J.J. Scullion & J. Reumann, 'Righteousness', *Anchor Bible Dictionary*, ed. D. N. Freedman (New York: Doubleday, 1992) Vol. 5 pp. 724–73

K. Stendahl, *Paul Among Jews and Gentiles* (London: SCM, 1976)

J. Ziesler, *The Meaning of Righteousness in Paul* (Cambridge University, 1972)

On Germany:

The chief source of the historical parts of the chapter is Klaus Scholder's *The Churches and the Third Reich* (London: SCM, 1987–88). This is a magnificent and very detailed study in two volumes which goes up to 1934 only, owing to the untimely death of the author.

The most relevant book of Dietrich Bonhoeffer is his *No Rusty Swords* (London: Collins, 1965). There is a fascinating book edited by Eberhard and Renate Bethge and Christian Gremmels, entitled *Dietrich Bonhoeffer: A Life in Pictures* (London: SCM, 1986), and a short biography by Renate Wind, *A Spoke in the Wheel: The Life of Dietrich Bonhoeffer* (London: SCM, 1991).

On Duchrow see his *Global Economy: A Confessional Issue for the Churches?* (Geneva: WCC Publications, 1987), and *Europe in the World System 1492–1992* (Geneva: WCC Publications, 1992).

On Japan:

Books on Japanese Christianity are not so plentiful in the West. One of the best sets of essays on the Emperor System is in the *Bulletin of the Commission on Theological Concerns of the Christian Conference of Asia* (December 1982). On Christianity in Japan in the last twenty years see *Christianity in Japan 1971–90*, edited by Kumazawa Yoshinobu and David L. Swain and published by Kyo Bun Kwan (The Christian Literature Society of Japan), Tokyo in 1991.

On Britain:

William Temple, *Christianity and Social Order* (Penguin, 1942)
Faith in the City: A Call for Action by Church and Nation (London: Church Publishing House, 1985)
Eamonn Butler, *Hayek* (London: Temple Smith, 1983)
Malcolm Alison & David L. Edwards, eds., *Christianity and Conservatism* (London: SPCK, 1991) (Contains Mrs Thatcher's address to the Church of Scotland General Assembly)
Hugo Young, *One of Us: A Biography of Margaret Thatcher* (London: Macmillan, 1989; Pan paperback, 1990)
Brian Griffiths, *Morality and the Market Place* (London: Hodder & Stoughton, 1980)
Brian Griffiths, *The Creation of Wealth* (London: Hodder & Stoughton, 1984) (Griffiths was Special Adviser and Head of the Policy Studies Unit at 10 Downing Street from 1985)

For critics of the Thatcher years, see Ronald H. Preston, *The Future of Christian Ethics* (London: SCM, 1987) chapters 8 and 9, and Kenneth Leech, 'The Christian Critique of Thatcherism', in Andrew Linzey & Peter Wexler, eds., *Fundamentalism and Tolerance: An Agenda for Theology and Society* (Bellew Publishing, 1991).